HARRY MAURER

On Your Own, But Not Alone!

50 FREE and Low-Cost Resources for Entrepreneurs and Small Businesses!

First published by On Cue Productions 2019

Copyright © 2019 by Harry Maurer

All rights reserved. No part of this publication may be reproduced, stored or transmitted in any form or by any means, electronic, mechanical, photocopying, recording, scanning, or otherwise without written permission from the publisher. It is illegal to copy this book, post it to a website, or distribute it by any other means without permission.

Harry Maurer has no responsibility for the persistence or accuracy of URLs for external or third-party Internet Websites referred to in this publication and does not guarantee that any content on such Websites is, or will remain, accurate or appropriate.

Designations used by companies to distinguish their products are often claimed as trademarks. All brand names and product names used in this book and on its cover are trade names, service marks, trademarks and registered trademarks of their respective owners. The publishers and the book are not associated with any product or vendor mentioned in this book. None of the companies referenced within the book have endorsed the book.

Some links provided are affiliate links, which means that if you choose to upgrade to a paid plan, I will earn a commission. This commission comes at no additional cost to you. I believe in these resources and recommend them because they are helpful and useful, not because of the small commissions I may make if you decide to upgrade.

First edition

This book was professionally typeset on Reedsy.
Find out more at reedsy.com

*To my wife Carol Ann who always encourages me to be the best I can be.
I love you!*

Contents

Introduction   iv

I   The Neccessities

1. GOOGLE VOICE - Your Own Voicemail System   3
2. GOOGLE PROGRAMS & SERVICES - A Quick Note...   9
3. GOOGLE DOCS - Includes FREE Text Transcriptions!   12
4. NEXTIVA - Your Business Switchboard   15
5. HUBSPOT - A Contact Management Software   17
6. CANVA - Design Graphics Like a Pro!   21
7. PLACE-IT - Another Design Tool!   23
8. MAILER LITE - An Autoresponder with Impressive Features   25
9. NINITE - The Easiest Way to Load Software   28
10. GET EMAIL - Need to Find Someone's Email Address?   31
11. FAXAWAY - The Economical Fax System   33
12. BENCHMARK EMAIL - Autoresponder and Integrated CRM   35
13. REEDSY - Need to Write a Book?   37
14. NAME SILO - Get Your Site Regstered...cheap!   40
15. BLOGGER - More than Just a Digital Diary   44

II   More Amazing Tools

16 SOCIAL BFF – Building Contacts on LinkedIn	49
17 SHORTKEYS – Saving You Keystrokes	51
18 123 FORM BUILDER – A Reliable Form Builder	54
19 NINJA FORMS – Forms for your WordPress Site	57
20 CALENDLY – Schedule your Calls, Meetings or Events	59
21 WEBINAR PRESS – How About a Free Webinar System?	62
22 ZOOM – Another way to "Webinar"	65
23 KUNAKI – CD's & DVD's for Products or Promotions	68
24 GUMROAD – The Easiest Way to Sell Your Products Online	71
25 FETCHAPP – Deliver Your Digital Purchases FREE!	75
26 KING SUMO – Create A "Viral" Contest to Build Your List…	78
27 ADD THIS – Spread the Word About Your Company!	82
28 ELEMENTOR – Build Your WordPress Website Yourself!	84
29 POP-UP ALLY – Grab Visitors Before They Leave!	86
30 MEMO CHIMP – Add a "Sticky-Note" to your Website!	88
31 BRITE VERIFY – Keep Your Mailer Reputation High!	90
32 ENABLE MEDIA REPLACE – An Easy Way to Make WordPress…	93
33 PHOTOPAD – Altering your Images can be a Breeze!	95
34 ANIMOTO – Quick Short Videos in Seconds!	98
35 OPENSHOT – Slick Video Editing	101
36 EVENTBRITE – Free Event Notifications!	103
37 TICKET TAILOR – Ticketing for Live Events!	105
38 LAST PASS – Never Forget a Password	109
39 ZAPIER – Let Your Programs Talk to Each Other!	112
40 FUNNELYTICS – See, Map and Plan Your Process!	115
41 FUNNEL BUILDER – The Smartest Marketing Tool in Your Kit!	118
42 TRELLO – Get Organized and Plan your Business…Visually!	122
43 TODOIST – Get Things Done!	124
44 BUBBL.US – Brainstorming Made Simple!	126
45 WHITESPARK – 3 tools to Advance your Google Reach	128

46	62 STOCK IMAGE SITES - Images at Your Fingertips!	131
47	PHOTOFUNIA - A Way to be Creating and Fun!	133
48	POSTER MY WALL - Professionally Designed Posters, Videos &...	135
49	WAVE VIDEO - Create Short Promotional Videos!	138
50	WONDERSHARE STREAMING - Don't Waste Your Most Productive...	140

In Conclusion...	144
Review Request	146
About the Author	147

Introduction

I started collecting these resources for my own business, and although I have many programs that I pay top dollar for, I do what any new business proprietor, solo business owner or entrepreneur would do: Before I invest a lot of money in something I "think" I might need, my first step is to research and find a low-cost solution to my problems and I test them out to see if they will solve the problems that I am trying to solve.

At times, the programs I find are too simplistic, unreliable, or too cumbersome to warrant using them, but there are many times when I find amazing programs that allow me to accomplish exactly what I need to do, and many of these programs I still use today in my business. (Because I think they are great!)

On a side note, I am also involved with helping a number of non-profit organizations run campaigns economically. Because they have limited financial resources, I set them up with systems and programs that allows them to meet their needs — and they have been shocked and thrilled at what they have been able to accomplish at little or no cost!

I have tested these programs and services that I am recommending and have determined that the resources I am including in this book are extremely suitable for both new and established businesses.

Some of these programs and services may sound familiar to you, but I think you will be surprised at the free and low cost options they offer!

I decided to publish them here because even if you had an idea of what you were looking for, it would take you weeks of research to find the right programs and hours of time testing them to see if they will meet your needs — and even then, there would be many programs that you would have discarded, and others you would never have found on your own.

Did you know, for example, that you can get a free local phone number to use as a business line that will transfer calls to any phone you would like (even your cell phone!)?

Best of all, with a little forethought, that number can be designated as a "24 Hour Information Line" allowing callers to hear a short presentation about your company, store or service. Callers can even leave a message for you that will be transcribed as text and emailed to you! — and it's completely Free!

But don't think that because services like these are FREE that they are not high quality or dependable programs – far from it!

Most of these programs are free for two major reasons:

- A few of them are the "starter" versions of their main paid programs that may have limited or fewer features than their pricier options but are still suitable for business needs. For example, "Popup Ally" (mentioned in this book) only allows you to make two different signup forms with their Free version, but other than that, it works just as well as their Pro $99/year version.

- Another reason they are Free (or very inexpensive) is because the companies are confident that their services are the best and they know that if you try their programs or service and it helps your business grow, then when you are successful and ready (with lots of clients, prospects and sales), you will consider upgrading to one of their more robust plans!

And why not! Their service has worked well for you, you understand them and are indoctrinated into their system and with everything in place — why not simply upgrade and continue using a more advanced version of a program you are already accustomed to using?

And if you are a non-profit organization you will find that some of these companies are extremely considerate to groups like yours!

For example, Ticket Tailor (an online ticketing platform also featured in this book) gives non-profit organizations 20% off their already low event fees, and Animoto (a video making program) with approval of your 501(c)3 status, will allow you FULL ACCESS to their program FREE – all because they want to help non-profit organizations succeed!

Any smart company or organization will try to save money wherever they can, and finding helpful resources like these are invaluable!

Since most of these services are FREE, you risk nothing to implement them into your business. If you don't like them, you can easily move onto something else. But I believe that having features like these in your business as you grow will keep you efficient, help you maintain a professional image, and give you very impressive high-end tools that will allow your business to run smoothly!

Let me give you an example...

If you were a small community theater and used just TWO of these suggested programs – "Ticket Tailor" for online ticketing and "Vertical Response" for your newsletters or eblasts — you will have saved yourself over $1,500 per month! — That's over $18,000 a year!

Don't believe me?

Here's the breakdown for a theater with 4 events each month in a 250 seat theater with a ticket price of $20 per person...

- **Online Ticketing:**
    Ticket Tailor's price = $25/month (with no ticketing fees!) — vs EventBrite's price of $1,490 (for 4 events)

- **Email Promotions:**
    Vertical Response = FREE — vs Constant Contact's price of $31.50/month

That's just a one example of what you can save!

But as you may suspect, these programs are not just for non-profits – all businesses can benefit from these amazing resources!

I am excited to share these hidden gems with you!

I don't recommend instituting all of these service at once, but instead, I would select one or two at a time to incorporate into your business. Once you are happy with the results, then start adding others one-by-one as you see the need.

When you find a program in this book that you would like to consider, I would suggest marking the page so that you can easily find it later when you are ready to experiment with it.

As with anything on the internet, things change regularly and rapidly. Some of the free services that I really loved using changed their pricing structure recently and no longer have free versions. But as of this writing, all of my recommended resources in this book are either free or low-cost and are provided by companies that I trust will be around for a very long time.

Notice that with some programs I will provide you with an overview and suggestions for their use. In others, I will go into more detail and suggest how you might wish to set them up in ways to be the most effective for your business.

In most cases I will only be providing you with a short overview, so be sure to visit the product's web pages to understand each program in more detail – I know you're going to be truly stunned to see what they can do for you!

Here's to your success!

Harry Maurer

Entrepreneur / Marketer / Business Owner / All-around Nice Guy!

I

The Neccessities

For established businesses wishing to streamline their expenses — or for new businesses who want to get "up and running" as professionally as possible without spending an arm and a leg, these programs and services would be my <u>FIRST CHOICE</u> in helping those businesses succeed.

*

"'Someday' is a disease that will take your dreams to the grave with you. If it's important to you and you want to do it 'eventually,' just do it and correct course along the way."
— Tim Ferriss

1

GOOGLE VOICE - Your Own Voicemail System

https://voice.google.com/
FREE

This is my NUMBER ONE recommendation for any new business!

Using your home phone as a business line can make you come across as "unprofessional". Your wife or children answering the phone can be awkward – and clients leaving a message on a "home phone" can cause them to question the validity and professionalism of your business.

And using your cell phone as your main business line can be just as bad. You may not be prepared to talk to businesses when they call – you may be out with friends at a party, in a shopping mall or in your car. How professional does that sound to the person on the other end of the phone who is expecting to speak with a professional in your field?

Does that mean that you have to add an additional phone line to your existing home just for business?

Try "GoogleVoice" – it's FREE and they even GIVE you a local phone number!

I set GoogleVoice up — not just for myself — but for various groups and organizations I have worked with. It takes just a little configuring to set it up properly, but it is extremely useful and works great!

If you don't already have a dedicated phone line for your company or organization — or just want to add a "24 Hour Information Line" that people can call into 24 Hours a Day! — set up a GoogleVoice account!

I learned the concept of a "24 Hour Information Line" from professional marketing expert Joe Polish.

People are inherently distrustful of businesses and they are often shy. If they don't know you, customers may not want to speak with you personally… yet. Instead, they may just want to find out more about what you can offer them.

With that in mind, why not set this phone line up as a "24 Hour Information Line" that people can call into day or night and listen to a short presentation about your business or services? If they choose to, they can still leave a message for you and you can followup with them at the most appropriate time.

Here's how to set this up.

1. You must first establish a free Gmail account — If you don't already

have a Gmail account, you can set one up at **https://accounts.google.com/SignUp** .

If you already have a Gmail account and don't want to use it for business, just setup a second email account (you will be able to have phone messages sent elsewhere after you set this up)

2. After logging into your Gmail account, open the following link: **https://voice.google.com/u/0/signup**

3. Type in your area code and choose a phone number

4. Verify your number by entering a phone number of a phone you would like calls transferred to (you can alter this later). You can choose to have a verification code sent to you by text or you can opt to have the system call you with the verification code. Once you receive it, enter the code into the boxes provided.

5. You are now set to receive calls on your selected phone when someone calls your "Google Number"

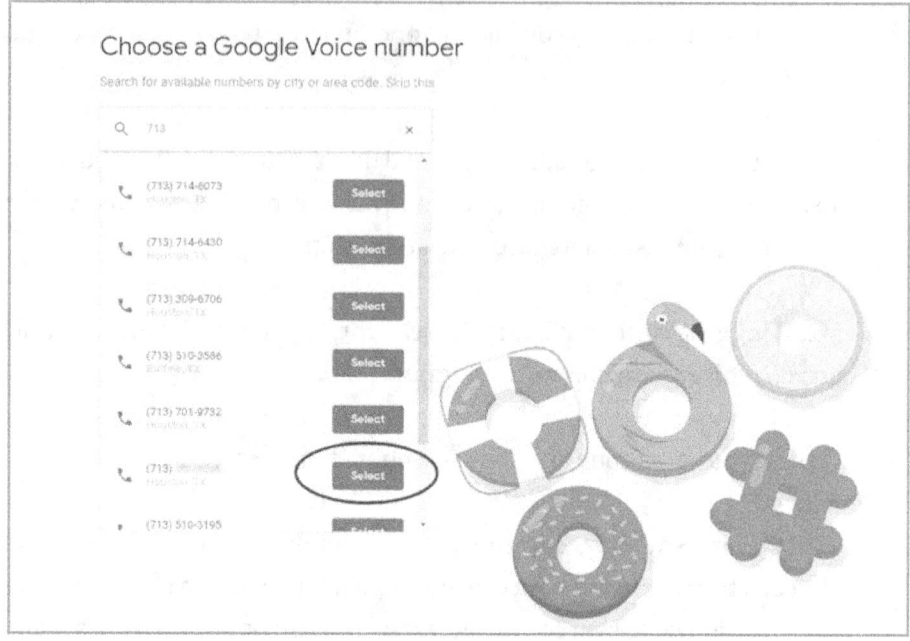

You can now dial your GoogleVoice number to check your voicemail, make a call, or change your Google Voice settings.

1. On your phone, call your Google Voice number.

2. During the greeting, tap Star (*).

3. Enter your PIN, and tap Pound (#).

4. To select an action, press the corresponding key:

- Check voicemail, if any: Tap 1.
- Make a call: Tap 2.
- Change your settings: Tap 4.
- Change your custom greeting: Tap 1.
- Record your name for standard greeting: Tap 2.

How easy was that?

Now let's configure it to use for your business.

There are many options you can choose from, so feel free to explore the options on the setup screen, but for our purposes, here is how I set it up for my own business and how I set this up for some of the non-profits that I work with.

I want the system to work as both an answering machine and a "24 hour Information Line" without ringing my phone. Instead, the system will allow callers to hear a short pre-recorded informative message abut my business and allow them to leave a voicemail message at the end of the promotional information. Their message will then be transcribed into text and immediately emailed to me so that I can either read or hear the message on my cell phone or desktop computer (with the aid of their Chrome app) and I can either call them back immediately or at a time where I will not be disturbed.

Here is how my outgoing message begins:

"Hello and thank you for calling [NAME OF COMPANY], this is [NAME]. We are the number one [30-60 SECOND SALES MESSAGE]... If you would like to leave a message, you may do so at the sound of the beep and we will return your call promptly. Thank you!" (beep)

Here's how to set it up:

1. Click on the gear icon on the top right of the page to go to "Settings"

2. On the Message Tab, turn the option "off" so that calls are not forwarded to your phone.

3. "Forward to email" should be in the on position.

4. You can record your message by either using your computer's microphone or by calling into the GoogleVoice number from your home phone.

Now here's how to have your messages sent to another (different) email address....

1. Log into the Gmail account you used to setup GoogleVoice: **https://mail.google.com**

2. Click on the Gear Icon ("Settings")

3. Click on the "Forwarding and POP/IMAP" tab

4. Under "Forwarding", choose "Add a Forwarding Address" and enter the email address where you would like your messages sent. (Note — I had difficulty setting this up with one non-profit organization whose email service forwarded emails to another address and it wouldn't work, so be sure to test this out with your email account. If it doesn't work, use another email account of yours).

***TIP:** In your email program you can filter just the voicemail messages by filtering emails from the following address:* **"voice-noreply@google.com"**

2

GOOGLE PROGRAMS & SERVICES - A Quick Note...

A quick side note here about "Google"...

For years I always believed that I NEEDED to use Microsoft products because I have a PC and Microsoft products were the industry standard.

Having worked with computers since the earliest days of "home computers", I quickly began to understand that whatever program you started with — then that is the program that you are dedicated to and will use.

That's why people latch onto Microsoft Office products. It is the same reason why people latch onto iPhones, and certain graphic programs — because it does a great job for them, they are highly rated, they are used to working with them, and it is what they started out with.

My first Word Processing program was called "WordStar" which, at the time, was a leading word processing program — and it was great.

When Microsoft Word came out, I was reluctant to switch, but when I did, I began to realize that it did the same thing in the same way and even had a similar look and feel as my WordStar program.

I have had an iPhone for years and when I made the decision to switch to an Android phone, I discovered that I could do the same things — and sometimes even better with it than with an iPhone (I know you iPhone users will argue with me on that!)

Some of the PAID online programs I use started incorporating GoogleDocs as their Word Processor (GoogleDocs is a FREE online software from Google).

When I started using GoogleDocs I realized I could get things done just as quickly, and the documents looked just as great as they did in Microsoft Word, and unlike static word processing programs, my documents were stored online automatically for me in my online Google Drive, so they were always available to me wherever I went — on any of my computers, on the road, on my tablet and even on my phone!

Although I doubt I would write something like a book on GoogleDocs (although I know people who have), it does what I need it to do to produce my letters and documents.

What I am trying to say is that that don't be so sure that you need to have certain programs. Google has FREE "state-of-the-art" programs that if I were starting out today with a limited budget, I would consider using.

Programs that include:

- **GoogleDocs** — A very good word processor that can read and save in standard Word Format.

- **Google Sheets** - A spreadsheet Program similar to Excel.

GOOGLE PROGRAMS & SERVICES - A QUICK NOTE...

- **Google Slides** - Comparable to PowerPoint.

- **Gmail** - A terrific email platform (that can also retrieve email from your other accounts as well!).

- **Google Calendar** - I switched over to this calendar long ago!

- **Google Chrome** - My web browser of choice (with lots of integrated apps).

- **Google Forms** - Design forms and quizzes!

- **Google Drive** — A space where you can store 15GB of files that you can access anywhere — and it's free!

Now, you certainly don't have to listen to me or take my recommendations, but there was a time when none of these programs were available, and if you needed a good word processor... and a spreadsheet program... and some sort of presentation software... and a calendar program... and a storage device...

...It would have cost you THOUSANDS of dollars! (and you would have to upgrade the software regularly).

These are all FREE! (And no software upgrades are needed!)

As a new business owner trying to save money, I would start by using Google programs and services and save my money to promote my business.

Because you know what?... Google is not going anywhere anytime soon.

3

GOOGLE DOCS - Includes FREE Text Transcriptions!

https://docs.google.com
FREE

So here's one of the reasons I went on a rant about Google programs...

GoogleDocs is a highly rated Word Processing program that has features that other word processors lack.

For example — Do you hate typing?

How would you like to simply "talk" into your computer and have it type everything you say?

You could purchase a copy of "**Dragon Naturally Speaking**" for about $150... or you can simply use the FREE GoogleDocs!

Here's how it works:

When you login to GoogleDocs and open a blank document, just click on the tab labeled "Tools" and select the option "Voice Typing" and a microphone icon will appear.

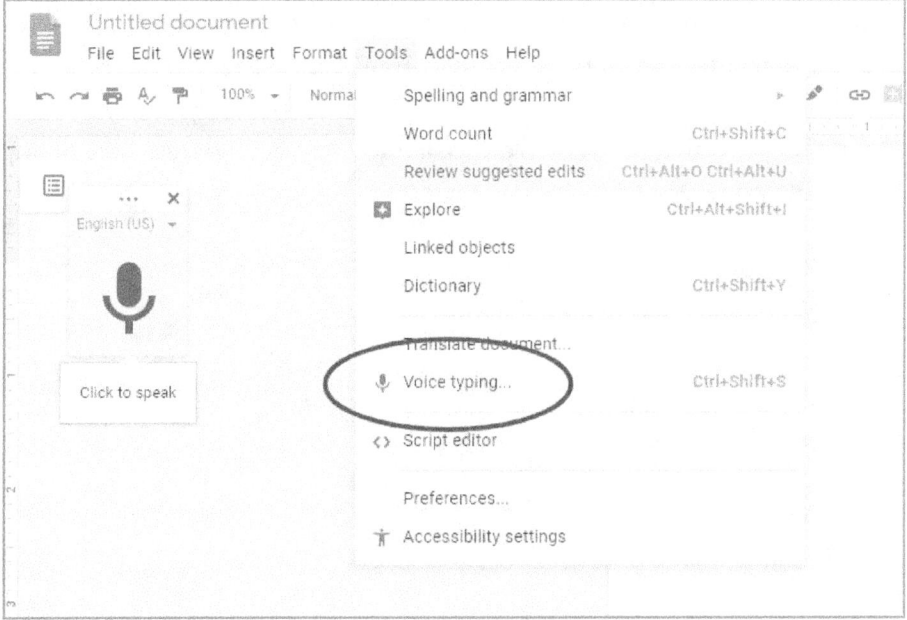

Click on the microphone icon and it will turn red, and then using your computer's microphone, just start speaking into our computer's microphone and you will see the program automatically type exactly what you say!

There are phrases you can say to end sentences and to add punctuation and formatting, like: "Period", "Comma", "Exclamation point", "Question mark", "New line", "New paragraph", etc..

It is easy to use and easy to understand and you can pause the recording at anytime by clicking once again on the microphone icon. And if you ever need help, just say, "Voice commands help" and help will appear! It is very accurate and, amazingly enough, it even works in different languages!

It works on your mobile phone too by using the mobile version of GoogleDocs, so you can dictate a letter or document nearly anywhere and have it transcribed into text!

And since Google Documents are saved online automatically in your free "Google Drive", you can dictate your document on your phone from the road, and then open it later when you get to your office!

I know people who have written **entire books** by using the free voice typing feature of GoogleDocs!

4

NEXTIVA - Your Business Switchboard

https://www.nextiva.com/free.html
FREE

Okay, I have to admit that I have not used this service because I am already using something similar that I have had for years, but I was recently introduced to Nextiva and I think that what they are offering is very impressive!

Ever since house phones and cell phones have included free nationwide calling, having your own 800 number (or 888 number) is not as important or "sexy" as it used to be, but having this as your answering service and switchboard can be very beneficial — especially if you are more than a "one-man" organization. Best of all, it is free to signup, there are no monthly fees, no setup fees and no contracts and you can cancel their service at anytime — so you really have nothing to lose!

You are provided with 100 minutes of inbound calls per month free. Any additional time after that is charged at 4.5 cents/minute , so you only pay for inbound calls that go over your 100 minutes a month plan.

The advantage of using this service is that it allows you to have virtual "extensions" that will allow callers to reach different people in your organization by pressing a button on their phone — even if they are in different areas of the country.

For example, if you are a home based business with partners or subcontractors in a different state, this one number will allow callers the option to be directed to the right person at the push of a button. And like GoogleVoice, voice messages are forwarded to you by email or text.

If you have more than one person or more than one department in your organization and you are a "virtual company" with people in different locations, this "switchboard" option may be something you might want to explore.

5

HUBSPOT - A Contact Management Software

https://www.hubspot.com
FREE (For up to 1,000,000 contacts!)

This is almost IDENTICAL to a paid system I am currently using – and they are offering it to you FREE to use with up to a MILLION contacts!

A Contact Relationship Management system (CRM) is an effective way to keep track of prospects and clients. In fact — I would say it is vital for your business to succeed!

When I first started marketing my services, I would keep track of every phone call, every letter and every email that I would send or receive from prospects.

The simplest way (and the way I teach new business owners who are not "tech-savvy") is to keep all of the information on file cards and date each interaction they have with a prospect on the card. When a customer would say to call them back in a month, I would file the card under the next month's tab, and by using a simple system like this, very few things fell through the cracks.

Then a variety of contact management software arrived on the scene, and although they were expensive, they were a high-tech way of doing pretty much the same thing with the added advantage of being able to send emails right from the program and a copy would always be accessible to you inside the software. Reminders could also be programmed to appear and notes from your calls or activities could be recorded.

I began by using "Contact Plus", then "Sidekick", then "Microsoft BCM", then 4 different iterations of "ACT!", before I moved to "Zoho" (I think you can tell that I was not thrilled with any one of them), and being a very visual person, I experimented with both "Pipedrive" and a similar program called "Salesmate" that I have now been using for more than a year.

I discovered that I was much more visually oriented, and for my needs, Pipedrive and Salesmate worked well with my style because they gave me a visual representation of where my prospects are in my sales process by creating a visual "Deal Pipeline" that looks just like file cards stacked in rows so that I can instantly see what the next step in my sales process should be, and with my mouse, I can drag a prospect from one stage in the pipeline to the next. Both programs will also post activities that I create onto my Google Calendar so that I don't miss meetings, calls or activities.

HUBSPOT - A CONTACT MANAGEMENT SOFTWARE

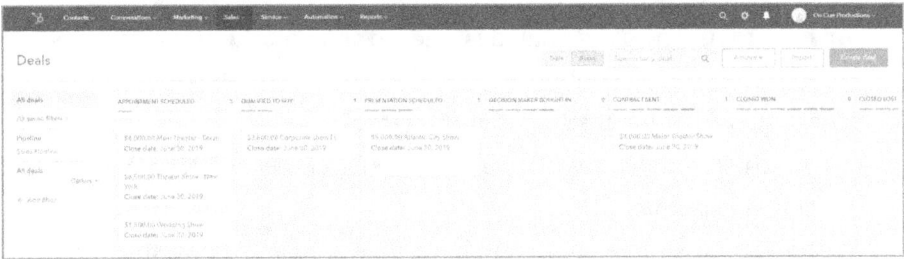

HubSpot's "Deals" Screen

HubSpot CRM works the same way and is designed similarly to Pipedrive and Salesmate. Best of all, it is free forever for your entire team to use, with an unlimited amount of data and you can enter up to 1,000,000 contacts!

Their thinking is: *"Don't pay for what you won't use. Start using a CRM that's free."*

Like Pipedrive and Salesmate, they also have a mobile app so that you can keep your contacts handy and work from the road.

Be warned though that although its basic CRM is completely free, that they have "add on hubs" that can cost money. Also, if you connect your email account (which is recommended) be sure to use your business account as any emails that come in will be automatically entered into HubSpot as a contact (they can be sorted and deleted later).

The more I delve into Hubspot the more impressed I am. HubSpot also has a wonderful series of training videos online that will allow you understand their system and help you learn to market your business and build your sales process, and if you decide it is worth it to use any of their add-on hubs, you can do that at anytime.

Some of the amazing features they have built into their system for FREE that many other CRM's do not, include:

- An easy to use graphic email designer to send marketing messages and newsletters out to clients.
- The ability to send meeting invites by email.
- A way to communicate with contacts through Facebook Messenger (from right inside of HubSpot).
- A code you can put on your site that will let you know how many times a contact has visited your website.
- Subscription forms and pop-up forms for your website.
- And even a "Live Chat" feature for your website where people can ask you questions right from your site!

Those are just a few of the included features — but don't be overwhelmed, you can add these and other features as you feel the need.

For the sake of comparison, Salesmate costs $144/year (www.salesmate.io) and Pipedrive costs $290/year (www.pipedrive.com).

As I said, they are both great programs and I recommend them highly, but if you are just starting out in business, it may be "overkill" to spend money until you are ready and know that it is something you will use — and like me, you may have to go through different programs until you find one that you are satisfied with.

But honestly, after using HubSpot, you may not want to switch to another CRM. HubSpot is a very impressive system to keep track of your interactions with prospects and clients. Although it has some limited features, it has some amazing ones as well. I would encourage you to see if it will meet your needs.

It is definitely worth trying out!

6

CANVA - Design Graphics Like a Pro!

www.canva.com
FREE

This has been a major online graphics design site for small businesses since its launch in 2012.

Rather than relying on complicated and expensive graphics software to create professional promotional images, Canva is a FREE program that makes it easy to put together your own designs.

And your choices are almost unlimited!

From book covers, to letterheads, to flyers and posters, to social media headers, postcards, greeting cards, coupons, logos, and so much more —

Canva makes the design process easy and your results professional!

A Sample Coupon Flyer!

Working with their online design program is very intuitive, but you should know that their templates do contain some "premium" images and if you would like to use those images in your design you will have to pay a small fee — but if you use the supplied free images in your designs, or if you import your own photos or images to complete your designs, you don't have to pay a thing!

So why purchase an expensive graphics program and go through the long learning curve to design materials you need to run your business?

Use Canva to easily create images and marketing materials to get your business up and running!

7

PLACE-IT - Another Design Tool!

*Place*it

https://placeit.net/
Prices vary from $2 - $9 (average) and more (priced per graphic piece)
Subscription available for $29/month

This can become your "go-to" marketing tool to design everything from professional flyers, banner ads, book covers, logos and more!

Although I think Canva is a wonderful online design tool, sometimes your design skills or lack of creativity can get in the way of expressing your message to the public. PlaceIt is filled with great creative and professional layouts all ready to adapt to your needs.

Need a logo? You can literally design one in 60 seconds!

Now, unlike Canva, none of the images you create are yours free — you have to pay to download them, but designing the marketing materials and saving them online are free.

When you are finally ready to download your finished masterpiece, PlaceIt will charge you to download it — but as far as I have experienced, their fees are quite fair — usually under $10 each.

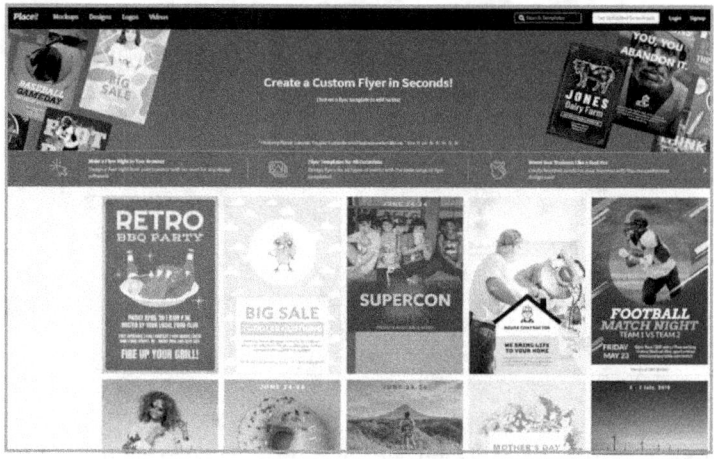

Among other amazing features, PlaceIt even has layouts for unusual needs like album covers, magazine covers, Facebook, YouTube and Twitter headers — and even T-shirt and coffee cup designs!

You can spend hours of amazement going through everything that is available!

If you like the idea of creating easy to design promotional videos — it even makes those as well!

Although their prices vary from project to project, they are all very economical (and they are extremely fun to play around with!).

I really think you may never need a professional designer — the program is THAT good!

8

MAILER LITE - An Autoresponder with Impressive Features

https://www.mailerlite.com/
FREE for up to 1,000 unique subscribers!

MailerLite is an advanced autoresponder system with some very impressive features.

Like any autoresponder system, it will allow you to send broadcasts and sequential emails to subscribers. But what sets it apart is its ability to "automate" emails based on a prospect's interaction with your email.

For example, if a prospect clicks on a link in your email for a certain product or service, the system can automatically send them an email (or series of emails) about that particular product or service. If a prospect does not open an email, the system can be designed to "re-send" the same email to them again at a later time (a process that usually has to be programmed manually).

It may sound confusing, but fortunately they make the process very simple to understand with a visual "tree" so that you can see what will happen each step of the way.

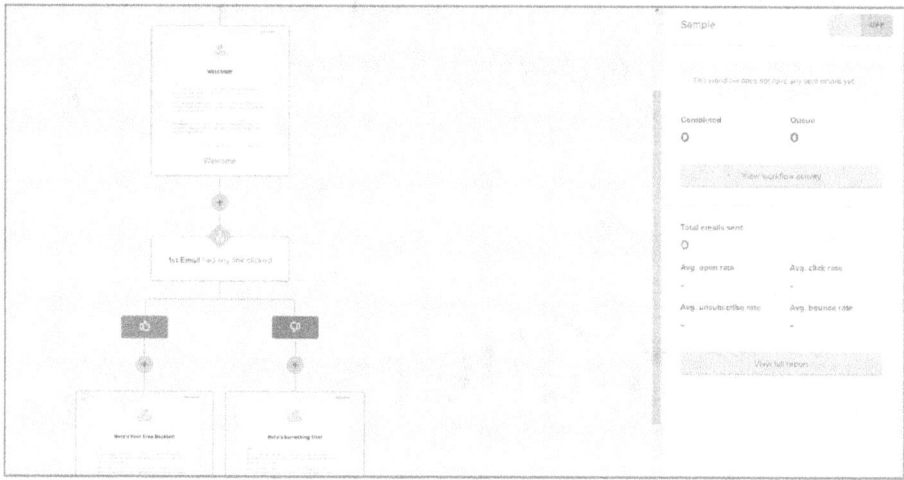

Think of the process in terms of "if/then" statements. If a prospect does "this action" than the program does "that action".

Other impressive features include:

- **A Built-in Landing Page Builder** — MailereLite provides both the templates and the web space to design your own landing page compete with your own personalized web address (so there is no domain required!) — a great option for beginning businesses which can also be used for specific products or projects. The landing pages are mobile responsive, GDPR compliant (a requirement for European online commerce) and they come with search engine optimization tools. You even have the ability to embed that landing page directly onto your Facebook page!

- **Pop-Up Forms** — Rather than just providing you with static sign-up forms as most autoresponders provide, MailerLite can also produce "pop-up" subscription forms that you can integrate into your own website.

Their "Forever Free Plan" only allows you up to 1,000 contacts and 12,000 emails per month, but if you are just starting out and are just building your list — or if you currently have less than 1,000 contacts, it will make the process of email marketing so much easier and less expensive for you!

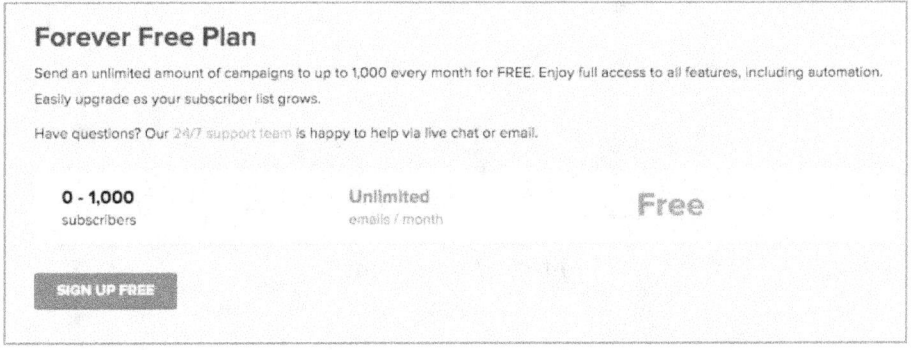

And once you reach 1,000 subscribers the pricing is still very reasonable at only $15/month for up to 2500 subscribers, $30/month for up to 5,000 subscribers, then $50/month for up to 10,000 subscribers.

Autoresponders are vital to any business's marketing efforts and finding one that is both feature rich, economical and reliable is rare.

I use MailerLite for some of my projects and it works extremely well.

9

NINITE - The Easiest Way to Load Software

https://ninite.com/
FREE

This BLEW ME AWAY when I was first introduced to this!

Do you need to install a PDF reader? A good free AntiVirus software? How about a compression program to create "zip" files – or maybe you need to install Chrome, DropBox, an image editor or a CD Burner?

You can find and install these programs on your own "one-by-one", but Ninite is a site that allows you to choose the software you want to install, then it automatically finds the right version for your particular computer and installs the programs you choose all at once for you!

NINITE - THE EASIEST WAY TO LOAD SOFTWARE

During my last visit they had over 80 free programs that were all highly rated by computer magazines.

Some of the programs I've installed and that I use on a regular basis include:

- **Chrome**: Web Browser
- **7-Zip**: a program to zip and unzip compressed files
- **Greenshot**: A program to capture screenshots
- **Skype**: Communications Program
- **AVG**: Virus Protection
- **Malewarebytes**: Malware scanner
- **LastPass**: Password Vault
- **Dropbox**: Online Storage
- and a lot more!

There is no need to search for each program's website online one by one, download the software from each site (hoping you are selecting the right version of the software for your computer and hoping you are downloading from a "legitimate" site) and then having to install each program one at a time. Ninite does it automatically for you with the push of a button!

It's great way to add programs you need to your computer – and vital if you are just beginning to configure a brand new computer!

It's an AWESOME time saver!

10

GET EMAIL - Need to Find Someone's Email Address?

https://getemail.io/
FREE (for 10 searched a month)

Need to get in touch with someone but don't have their email address?

Use "Get Email" to find it!

This program does just what it implies – it uses advance algorithms to scan the internet to find email addresses of a person in a company in seconds.

Although the site claims to *"Find the email address of any professional in any company"*, admittedly, there are times when it just doesn't find it, but it does work most of the time if you just want to send an inquiring email out to someone.

They also provide a convenient Chrome app so you can search for an email address right from your browser.

Just so you understand — sending an inquiry to someone you do not know is not considered "Spam" — it is simply making contact or an introduction to someone. But if you start adding them to an autoresponder and begin sending a series of marketing messages to them without their permission, then you are crossing the line.

So this should not be used for spamming purposes – but using it to reach out to someone to introduce yourself or your service to them and to make an initial contact doesn't hurt!

11

FAXAWAY - The Economical Fax System

http://faxaway.com/
$12/year

Okay, you may think that faxes are outdated, but there are times when you need to receive copies of the original documents like contracts, receipts, drawings and more.

But for the limited times you will need it, do you really want to invest in an expensive monthly fax service, a separate phone line or fax machine?

I use FaxAway!

At only $12 per year it is handy for me to have so that I can receive faxes at the office or on the road.

Now I have to admit their signup process is a bit antiquated, but once you sign up you will get your own fax number which will allow people to fax documents directly to you and those faxes will arrive as attachments in your email inbox.

You also have the ability to send faxes out by email if you need to (at $0.11/minute in the US) by sending it as an email or an email with an attachment (PDF, Word Documents and many other formats) to your prospect's fax number in the following format: **[faxnumber]@faxaway.com**.

They also provide "fax broadcasting" (the ability to send faxes to a list of people at once) and "fax-back services" allowing your customers to receive important information about your company, product or service at a reasonable cost.

As I mentioned, it is handy for me to receive signed contracts, but I also use it to receive "fax-back" forms that I send out with my postal mailings providing an additional way for prospects to quickly and easily send me the information I need so that I can send them a quote for my services without them having to call me.

It does what I need it to do at a very small yearly cost.

12

BENCHMARK EMAIL - Autoresponder and Integrated CRM

https://www.benchmarkemail.com/
FREE for up to 2,000 contacts

With clients like **Toyota**, **Century 21**, **PBS** and **Re/Max**, you know that Benchmark is a reliable and respected email service!

I have a few different autoresponder services that I both use and that I recommend, and each has slightly different costs and features.

Benchmark is a great system and I have used it for a number of different projects.

Like other autoresponders, they provide you with hundreds of responsive email templates to use for broadcasts and automated emails designed with an easy to use drag-and-drop editor. You can design signup forms for your website quickly and easily and they have good customer support.

The additional feature they have is that they will also provide you with your own Customer Relationship Marketing system (CRM) to keep track of your interactions with your clients both offline and online in a way that integrates with Benchmark and with Gmail (via a Chrome extension). It is a very clean CRM system, but I will warn you, however, that with the free versions you are limited to only 250 contacts. After that, it is priced at $20/month (with a special pricing for subscribing to both Benchmark and their CRM together).

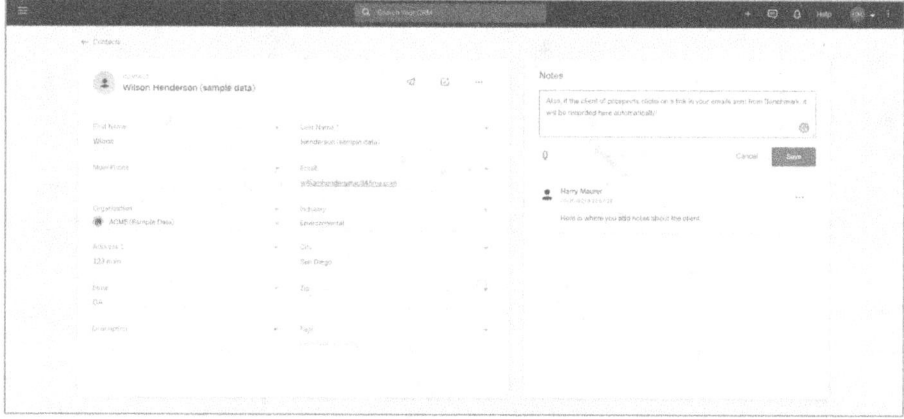

If you are just starting to use online marketing, or you have a small list of prospects and you are planning to use a Customer Relationship Marketing system anyway, this may be a good way to start.

If you love it, continue with their paid systems and you will be able to market online with a great autoresponder system, have a CRM that will automatically log prospect's interactions (clicks) with your Benchmark email campaigns and have the ability to keep notes and contact information about your clients handy with an easy to use CRM system.

13

REEDSY - Need to Write a Book?

https://reedsy.com
FREE

Okay — I'm giving away a secret here...

Yes, you can certainly write a book with MS Word or with GoogleDocs — or nearly any word processor. Heck — you can even write one with pen and paper! But there are tools that are designed specifically to make your writing and publishing job easier and without distractions.

Reedsy is a relatively new authoring program (developed in 2014) that will allow you a distraction-free area to write your book, your report or your "lead magnet" in an organized way.

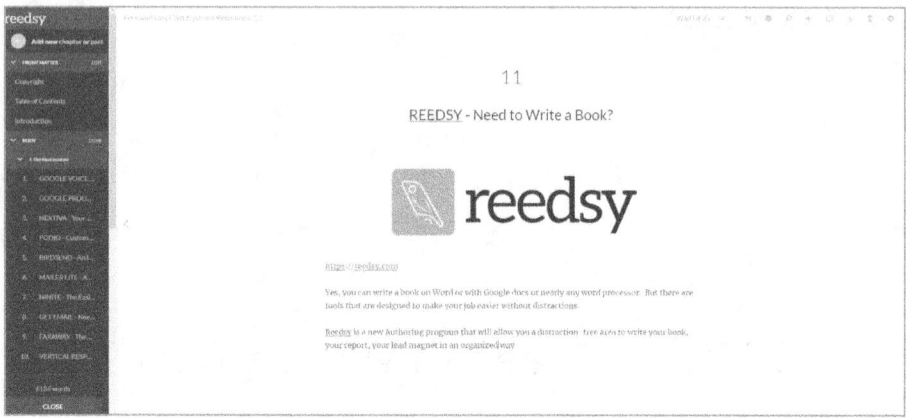

You don't need to think about formatting — just type your book in Reedsy, and when you are done it will format the book for you in a ready to print format automatically — complete with chapter headings, page numbers, table of contents and more!

Writing your book in chapters allows you to easily drag-and-drop chapters like blocks to reorganize them however you would like!

When you have finished writing and you are ready to publish you book as a "printed book", it will even format it for you for with just one click — essentially "typesetting" it for you in ready-to-go formats to send off to different publishing sites including Amazon KDP, the iBookstore and the Kobo Store.

It will also publish it quickly as a shareable PDF file if you would like.

Want to know how professional the results can be? You are holding a copy of a Reedsy publication in your hands right now!

I tried using this program as an experiment — and I have fallen in love with it!

You will be surprised at how quickly and how easily you can write, produce and publish a book too with the help of Reedsy!

14

NAME SILO - Get Your Site Regstered...cheap!

www.namesilo.com
$8.99/year

Every company needs to establish themselves on the internet, and having your own domain name is important for a number of reasons.:

1. Your domain name is your web presence.

2. It adds credibility and shows that you are serious about your business and plan to be around awhile!

3. It helps you when you promote your services in search engines.

4. With a domain email address, your emails will get through spam filters much easier than by using a "free" email service like Gmail, AOL, etc.

If you have experienced purchasing a domain name from other companies, you will find that the prices range pretty dramatically from $10 - $35 (and there are some unscrupulous companies that will try convincing you to pay as much as $79/year!).

I have many of my domains listed with GoDaddy, and I think their service has been terrific, but if I were to start again and I knew about NameSilo, I would definitely have used them!

A couple feature that I should point out is that they include both domain privacy and domain protection at no additional charge!

What is Domain Privacy?

According to ICANN regulations, every domain is required to be listed in a publicly accessible database called WHOIS, and over time that database has become a target for hackers and spammers.

Domain Privacy bi-passes this regulation and keeps that information secure by not immediately displaying your information. Instead, it directs all inquiries to "PrivacyGuardian.org" where they can submit a form requesting the information from NameSilo instead — a step that spammer will avoid.

What is Domain Protection?

Due to malicious attacks, it is possible for people and businesses to lose their domain name! Domain Defender provides 2-factor identification and security questions that have to be answered before any changes to your account can be made.

At only $8.99/year, it is a very small price to pay for domain registrations, and at that small cost, why not purchase additional names to target specific areas or markets?

COMPANY	PRICE	PRIVACY	PROTECTION	TOTAL	COMPARISON
NameSilo	$8.99	FREE!	FREE!	$8.99	You save with us!
GoDaddy	$15.17	$9.99	$5.00	$30.16	$21.17 more expensive
Namecheap	$10.87	$2.88	Not Offered	$13.75	$4.76 more expensive
Google	$12.00	$0.00	Not Offered	$12.00	$3.01 more expensive
Uniregistry	$10.88	$0.00	Not Offered	$10.88	$1.89 more expensive
Network Solutions	$34.99	$9.00	$0.00	$43.99	$35.00 more expensive
Register.com	$37.00	$11.00	Not Offered	$48.00	$39.01 more expensive
eNom Central	$39.95	$8.00	Not Offered	$47.95	$38.96 more expensive
Dynadot	$10.99	$2.00	Not Offered	$12.99	$4.00 more expensive
Dotster	$14.99	$8.99	Not Offered	$23.98	$14.99 more expensive
Yahoo	$9.95	$9.00	Not Offered	$18.95	$9.96 more expensive
Melbourne IT	$36.50	$15.00	Not Offered	$51.50	$42.51 more expensive
Fabulous	$29.95	$0.00	$0.00	$29.95	$20.96 more expensive
Moniker	$9.59	$4.00	$19.99	$33.58	$24.59 more expensive
Name.com	$12.99	$3.99	Not Offered	$16.98	$7.99 more expensive
Domain.com	$9.99	$8.99	Not Offered	$18.98	$9.99 more expensive
Gandi	$15.50	$0.00	Not Offered	$15.50	$6.51 more expensive
Hover	$13.17	$0.00	Not Offered	$13.17	$4.18 more expensive

*The above prices reflect standard pricing without promotion to register a .com domain on each of the associated web sites. We update this list frequently, however, if you find a mistake please let us know.

Say you are a flooring company and sell high-end carpet, tile and wood flooring in Dallas, Texas. You could purchase different names like:

- **CeramicTilesDallas.com**
- **CarpetDallas.com**

- **WoodFlooringDallas.com**

And when you determine that there is a need for a service you provide and you decide that you would like to promote a "carpet stretching service" (but don't want to dilute your main brand) you can purchase a domain called:

- **CheapCarpetStretchingDallas.com**

You may also have unrelated businesses or markets that you want to promote your business to and having separate online identities will avoid confusion.

But even if you are only looking to save money each year on your current domain name — NameSilo is a great service!

There are no hidden fees or upcharges — what you see is what you will pay, and if you transfer you domain to them, they will even add up to one additional year free!

15

BLOGGER - More than Just a Digital Diary

https://www.blogger.com
FREE

Creating a blog may seem like simply creating on "online digital diary", but there are so many great ways to use a "blog" in your business.

Blogs allow you to provide useful information that would not necessarily be found on your web page. After all, if you put everything you knew on your web page, it would be so cluttered that no one would ever read it!

But having an area where you can discuss industry changes, new product announcements, customer case studies, links to articles that you or your company are featured in, ways that your service or product can be used, and more is helpful and informative to people considering your company or service and can make you stand out among your competition.

Blogger was purchased by Google in 2003, and although Google's algorithms change regularly, it is safe to say that by posting useful information on your blog, you will position yourself well in Google and other search engines with answers to questions that customers are looking for.

According to Rocket Media (a digital marketing agency based in Arizona): *"blogging is one of the easiest, most cost-effective ways to improve your search rankings."*

And Blogger is simple to use. You simply select a template, design it so that it coordinates with your website or vision and then just start adding images and blog posts.

Can you design a blog with your current web design program? — Yes you can.

WordPress has a blog feature (in fact, WordPress was originally designed to create blogs), but it means that you have to log into your WordPress administration dashboard regularly to add new blog posts. I have also found that it is not easy to configure WordPress blogs to work with some WordPress themes and plugins.

Using Blogger is so much easier and since it is not self-hosted on your own domain where data can be lost, it is more convenient just to log into Blogger to add your posts.

A blog can really help people understand your business, your vision and your goals, and links to your posts can be sent to your email list through your autoresponder to keep clients informed and to keep your company "top of mind".

Blogger makes it easy to add information that will allow you to stand out from your competitors and rank higher in the search engines while helping your customers and prospects understand your business while at the same time giving you authority in your industry.

II

More Amazing Tools

Explore these treasures — they are hidden gems that can save you time, make you more productive, solve many problems and take your business to a new level.

*

"Spend time upfront to invest in systems and processes to make long-term growth sustainable."
-Jeff Platt

16

SOCIAL BFF - Building Contacts on LinkedIn

https://socialbff.io/
FREE for 100 visits/day

Do you do a lot of research on LinkedIn?

Want to get more people to visit your profile and find out more about you and your company?

I was introduced to this chrome add-in recently and was very impressed!

There is a paid version ($49/month), but their FREE version **automatically visits up to 100 LinkedIn pages a day** of people in categories you want to connect with in a way that does not "blacklist" you on LinkedIn.

What is the benefit of automatically visiting 100 LinkedIn pages?

Have you ever had people visit your LinkedIn page and not knowing who they were you visited their page in return to find out who they were?

You're not the only one!

This is a great way to get people to visit your LinkedIn page, and if your profile is well written, it can introduce you to them and encourage them to contact you and allow you to start a conversation with them.

In my first few times using this program and this tactic I made contact directly with decision makers.

This idea works!

17

SHORTKEYS - Saving You Keystrokes

https://www.shortkeys.com/lite.htm
FREE

This is the perfect addition to Social BFF – although I know you will also find it useful in other places as well!

ShortKeys is a program that allows you to create a "hotkey" by assigning keystrokes of your choosing (something you would not accidentally type, like "#li" or "//oo") and the program will type out a pre-written paragraph — or even an entire page of text for you instead!

For example, if you are using Social BFF and you decide to connect with someone on LinkedIn, rather than just clicking the "connect" button which not only is a lazy way to make contact with someone on LinkedIn (and many people tend to ignore those generic invitations), you use a "hotkey" instead, and with just 3 or 4 keystrokes a personalized message is entered that says:

"Hi # ,
   I saw your profile and would like to connect with you. After we connect, tell me more about your company and how I might be able to help you.
   Best Wishes – [YOUR NAME]"

You then just edit the text to your liking.

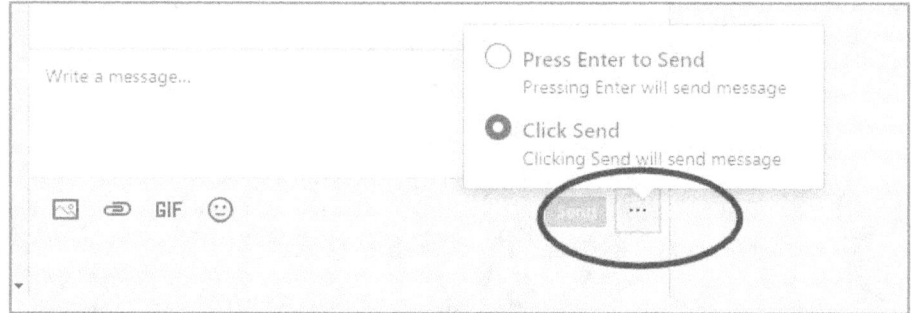

(Quick Tip for LinkedIn Users: Be sure to select the option "Click Send" so that as you edit the email, it will not be sent prematurely until you click the SEND button …)

ShortKeys works in any program — email programs, texts, word processors, and more!

It's also handy when you need to type "canned replies" to people, descriptions of your services, current pricing, and more.

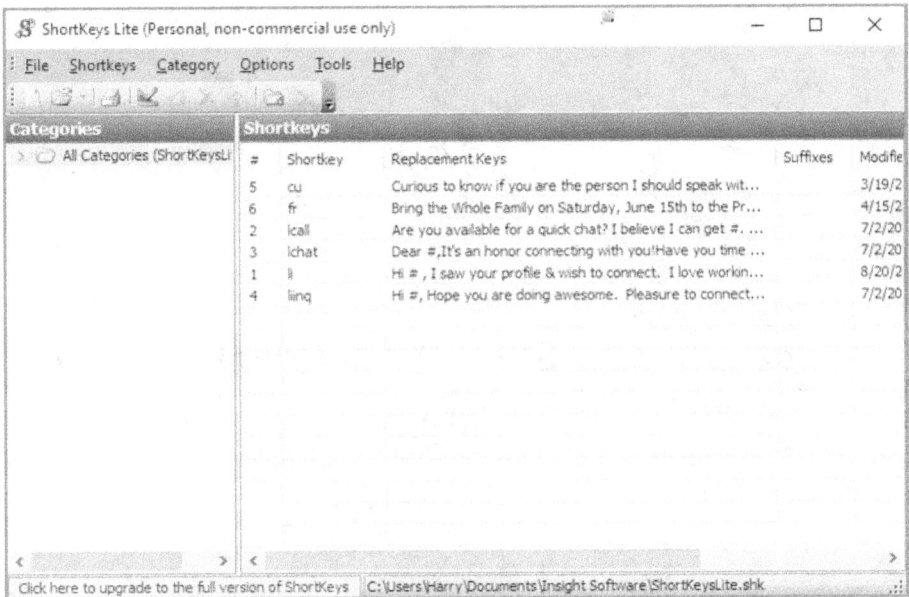

The free version allows you to program up to 15 keystroke combinations. If you decide that you really need more, the full version is only $29.95

18

123 FORM BUILDER - A Reliable Form Builder

www.123formbuilder.com
FREE for up to 5 forms with 10 fields each
(limited to 100 submissions per month)

I had such a difficult time finding a good and reliable "form" program — something that I could design a form with to use on my website that would allow people to enter their information into the form and then have the form sent to me.

It sounds like such a simple process, and I have tried TONS of free programs (and even some paid programs), but some were too complicated to setup and others were unreliable and I was often disappointed...

123 FORM BUILDER - A RELIABLE FORM BUILDER

...until I found "123 Form Builder".

Here's the "Bad News" — Their free version allows you to only make 5 forms and will only allow you to receive a total of 100 submissions a month. You are also limited to using only 10 entry fields per form.

The "Good News" is that it is easy to setup, easy to use and works flawlessly. And compared to their normal minimum pricing of $20/month — this FREE option is ideal for new businesses!

I am currently using this for my "Comment Forms" on some of my web sites. I also have used this to create inquiry forms that I use on certain landing pages of mine that will allow prospects to send information to me so that I can provide them with a quote for my services.

Having a form on your site will allow you to easily qualify people and allows you to receive their contact information and the information you require so that you can evaluate their needs in advance so when you phone them back, you are prepared and can provide them with the right options.

I think forms are invaluable tools.

19

NINJA FORMS - Forms for your WordPress Site

https://ninjaforms.com/
https://wordpress.org/plugins/ninja-forms/
FREE (WordPress Plugin)

Do you need a more complex form on your website?

Ninja Forms is a WordPress plugin that allows you to design forms for various purposes easily and quickly through a "drag-and-drop" interface with absolutely no coding skill required.

If your business requires information so that you can provide a quote, Ninja Forms the perfect way to collect that information.

Just put the form on your website and prospects can fill it out with all of the information you will require to send them an accurate quote.

It does take some configuring to get this to work properly with your email provider, but I have used this on some of my sites, and when configured properly, it works great!

20

CALENDLY - Schedule your Calls, Meetings or Events

https://calendly.com/
FREE for one event type

How many times have to tried calling people and couldn't reach them? And then perhaps they try calling you back and you were out of the office?

Playing "phone tag" is no fun and wastes everyone's time.

Calendly is a service that allows clients and prospects to schedule a call or an appointment with you during times that are most convenient for both of you.

Lately, this phone scheduling process is being used by consultants and businesses that would like to offer a "Free 30 Minute Consultation" with prospects. (An idea to consider!)

Calendly's scheduler is completely configurable providing customers with days and times that you will accept calls or appointments. It allows people to make an appointment right from a link on your website or from a link in an email with times that you determine you will be available.

Some of the free features include:

1. The ability to schedule an unlimited number of calls or events.

2. Your own personalized "link" to send to clients in an email or as a link on your website so people can schedule a call or meeting with you.

3. The scheduled event can be entered onto your calendar for you automatically (Google Calendar, Office 365, Outlook or iCloud).

4. Emails are instantly sent to both you and your client confirming the appointment.

Calendly normally costs $8/month for their least expensive "full-version" plan with all of the bells and whistles, but their free plan is quite good!

Now, after repeated attempts at reaching someone, I send an email with a link to my calendar to schedule a time for a quick phone call.

The limitation of Calendly's free version is that it only allows you to create one type of event (either a call, a meeting, an appointment or an event) — but even so, it extremely useful.

For example, wouldn't it be great if you could plan certain days of the week with only certain times available for calls or appointments?

Traditionally, I do my sales calls 3 days a week and my Calendly calendar is setup that way so I can group all of my business calls together during those times.

When someone books a time slot, it no longer appears as a selection on the calendar, so the next person has to select a different time slot.

If you are involved in sales (and what new business **IS NOT** involved in sales?) — or if you provide consultations or demonstrations, I think you will find Calendly very useful!

21

WEBINAR PRESS - How About a Free Webinar System?

https://www.getwebinarpress.com
FREE WordPress plugin

I am a big fan of webinars and I listen to them all the time. In fact, I often record them as audios and I listen to many of them in the car when I have more available time on my hands.

I produced webinars and "Video Sales Letters" (VSL's) for my own business and they have been very helpful in marketing my services.

A webinar allows you make a 30 minute or more presentation to a large group of people who have specifically signed up to hear it. It is more effective, and at times, more efficient than giving your presentation "one-by-one" to prospects. In many cases the webinar, once produced, can be automated to run whenever you want over and over again.

But webinar platforms are expensive! The leading industry platform is called GoToWebinar and can cost between $109/month and as much as $499/month.

Now if you have never presented a webinar...

- How do you know how effective it will be for your particular business?

- How do you know if you are the best presenter of your product or service?

- How do you work on developing the "perfect" presentation without laying out thousands of dollars as you try presenting webinars over and over again?

WebinarPress (Formerly known as "WP Webinar System") is a WordPress plugin that will allow you to create an unlimited number of webinars and connect with an unlimited number of attendees without paying a single penny!

And just like the major players, WebinarPress will send email notifications and regular reminders to those who sign up. You have the ability to style the webinar pages to your liking, and at the end of the presentation, you can download the attendee's contact information.

Their "Lite" version is Free, but if you would like other features that include the ability to produce "replays", "pre-recorded" webinars, "Just-In-Time" webinars, live chats and more, they price their service between $197 and $497/year. (Which is close to what the big boys charge PER MONTH!)

...But to put on your own live webinar in a professional format and test the waters — you can't beat FREE!

22

ZOOM - Another way to "Webinar"

https://zoom.us/
FREE for presentations running up to 40 minutes
with up to 100 participants

Although the Free version I am about to describe is not actually a "webinar" platform (for that you would have to pay $40/month), but here is another webinar option using the "meeting" option in Zoom.

Believe it or not, this conferencing program was originally designed by its founder Eric S. Yuan while he was attending college in China as a way for him to communicate with his girlfriend who lived 10 hours away!

Launched in 2011, Zoom — a video and communications platform, was released as a business application for meetings, video conferences and 1-on-1 presentations and later found a place as an alternative Webinar platform.

As I mentioned, their webinar platform is a paid service costing $40/month, but there is a workaround using their free "meeting" option.

Unlike a professional webinar system that will send out emails in advance and allow people to sign up, you will have to set that up on your own with a web page and an autoresponder which would allow people to "sign-up" and deliver the login information for you.

Other than that, the free version of Zoom is quite robust. The only major limitations you will have are that the presentation can only last up to 40 minutes in length and you can only have a maximum of 100 attendees.

But it's really easy to use!

You simply sign in, schedule when you would like the meeting (webinar) to be held, email the link they provide you with to your participants, and at the scheduled time you log in as the "host" of the meeting and start your presentation.

The presentation can be you on camera, various windows on your computer screen (including PowerPoint slides, videos or screen shares of any program that you can bring up on your computer) and you can even hand the webinar off to another participant in a remote location at the click of a button!

Another wonderful feature is that the attendees, if they choose to, can call in and listen to the presentation on their phones with a phone number that Zoom provides rather than watching the presentation on their computer.

And with the Zoom mobile app, attendees can not only watch the presentation on their mobile device, but the entire presentation can be presented by the host right from his or her mobile phone!

A unique feature that zoom has is that if you don't like the background of your office in the shot, it has a "green screen" option where you can use an image as a virtual background instead. You also have the ability to record the presentation (which you can later embed in a web page as a "replay").

If you don't have a WordPress site to use WebinarPress and would rather use a hosted platform with some additional features — using Zoom to present webinars is a great option.

23

KUNAKI - CD's & DVD's for Products or Promotions

https://www.kunaki.com/
Prices Vary - Approximately $2.00 each
for fully packaged CD's or DVD's with no minimums

If you ever needed professionally packaged CD's or DVD's — either as promotional items or as a product and you don't want to have to order 500 of them at a time — Kunaki is the perfect choice!

I would often use their service when I just need a small quantity of CD's. These can be CD's or DVD's containing software, music or videos — all professionally produced and packaged. And when I say "professionally packaged" — I'm not kidding! The CD's arrive just as if you purchased them from a store packaged in a traditional "jewel case" with full color printing on the CD, glossy inserts and the entire product is shrink-wrapped in plastic complete with a bar code!

Their prices do fluctuate, but at the time of this writing, their prices range between .40 cents each for the CD only (no case), or $1.10-$1.90 for the CD or DVD packaged in cardboard jackets, jewel cases or taller DVD cases (shrink-wrapped with printed inserts).

They also recently added unique and novel "Vinyl Records" as an option at $30 each.

With the popularity of videos, sending a promotional video or a product demonstration — or even a copy of your webinar or live presentation as a professionally packaged DVD to a client would be very impressive! — I even like the idea of just sending the audio of a webinar or teleseminar on CD for client to listen to in the car at a time when they can focus on your presentation without being disturbed!

Now, if you were going to order a large quantity of CD's, there are other companies I would probably recommend (like DiscMakers or Oasis CD), but for small orders, or to just "test the waters" with a marketing or promotional item, I would recommend trying Kunaki first before spending hundreds of dollars. Best of all, they will send you your first copy FREE so you can review it and see the quality for yourself!

Be aware though that with Kunaki, there are no sales people when you order. The ordering process is completely automated, but is not too difficult. Simply upload the data and then upload the designs for the case inserts and then you will see a visual representation of your product online. If you like it, you just order exactly the number of items you need — from as few as "1" to as many as you would like!

If you would like the product sent directly to your customers, they can do that as well.

...Although at $4.30 each for shipping, I think you can do better shipping it on your own as needed — especially if this is a promotional item that you would want to send along with promotional or collateral materials.

And if this is for a product you are selling, they even have an option to create a sales page for you at no charge so that customers can order directly online and the product is printed and delivered as they are ordered and money is sent directly to your PayPal account — no need to store CD's or take orders yourself!

So for small quantity CD's or DVD's — Kunaki is the way to go!

24

GUMROAD - The Easiest Way to Sell Your Products Online

https://gumroad.com/
FREE plan
($10 for more advanced features)

Do you sell digital goods, physical goods, software — or perhaps have a monthly newsletter subscription?

You may want to look at Gumroad to setup and sell those products.

- You can use Gumroad to sell physical products that you will mail out to customers.

- You can use Gumroad to sell and deliver digital products (like videos, software, ebooks and audio books).

- You can use Gumroad as a "membership site" to sell subscriptions (like a monthly newsletter or "tip-sheets").

And Gumroad will do all the the work for you — taking care of the sales page, the credit card processing, the monthly billing (for newsletter subscriptions), the digital delivery of the product, etc., and payments are sent right to your PayPal account!

Gumroad will even provide you with nicely designed ads and links to include on your web page and social media pages.

It is free to join and their more advanced features are $10/month for up to 1,000 customers each month.

Rather than having to go through PayPal, buyers can use nearly ANY credit card, and on their FREE plan, Gumroad will charge you 8.5%+.30 cents per transaction. (For paid plans, they charge only 3.5% + 30¢ per transaction). Naturally, you can roll those charges into your pricing.

8.5% may sound like a lot, but you **WILL NOT** be paying any PayPal fees — these are the only charges.

So, for example, when someone purchases my $15 digital product, I will receive $13.43 and not have to do a thing! — They provide the sales page, they collect the money, they send the digital product to the purchaser and they send the proceeds to my PayPal account.

It is completely "hands off"!

GUMROAD - THE EASIEST WAY TO SELL YOUR PRODUCTS ONLINE

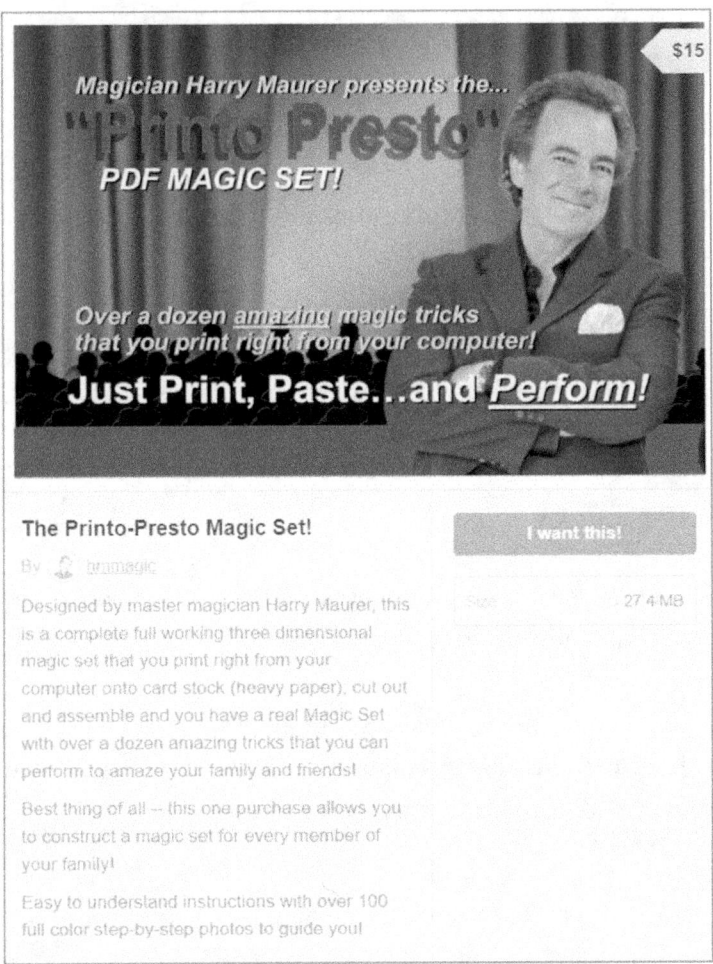

Some additional feature include:

- The ability to create "discount codes" for your clients (if you wish).

- The ability to generate "license keys" to unlock the digital product.

- Gumroad collects the names and email addresses of your customers for you.

- You can set up affiliate programs so that both you and your affiliates get paid.

- Gumroad provides product buttons and links that you can add to your website or social media pages.

- They provide you with your own web page ("Profile Page") that you can direct people to listing your products.

- You can even setup a product for a time limited "rental" instead of purchase.

- If you have a free digital product (something you are not charging for) Gumroad will deliver it for you at no charge!

Maybe at some point in your business you may want to invest in your own online store or membership site, but for all they provide you with in their sales platform — Gumroad is a great way to start!

25

FETCHAPP - Deliver Your Digital Purchases FREE!

https://www.fetchapp.com/pages/plans
FREE for 5MB of data storage and 25 sales per day

If you are just starting out selling digital products and have a report, an ebook or a digital product (music, photos, etc.) that totals less than 5MB in size, you may want to look at FetchApp.

Unlike Gumroad, they do not provide you with a sales page or pop-ups — this is strictly a delivery service for your digital goods.

FetchApp's free plan allows you to store up to 5MB of data and allows you to make up to 25 sales per day at no charge!

Once you have achieved 25 sales per day, and if your digital product is priced well, then moving onto their paid plan is a no-brainer.

For example: If your product is priced at $27, rather than paying a percentage of each sale — 3.5% for example that Gumroad charges (which amounts to approximately .95 cents per sale or $24 for each 25 orders), it would be less expensive to move onto their paid plan costing only $5/month which would also increase your data space to 50MB and will allow you an <u>unlimited</u> number of sales!

Here is a partial list of their pricing:

| Pricing | Storage | Bandwidth |
Monthly	Monthly*	Monthly**
Free	5 MB Storage Space	Limit 25 orders per day
$5 Monthly	50 MB Storage Space	Unmetered Bandwidth
$10 Monthly	Use your own (details)	Use your own (details)
$10 Monthly	2 GB Storage Space	Unmetered Bandwidth
$20 Monthly	5 GB Storage Space	Unmetered Bandwidth
$30 Monthly	10 GB Storage Space	Unmetered Bandwidth

Their next plan gives you 2 GIGABYTES of storage.

If you reach a point where you need more that 2GB of storage, another economical option they offer is for you to store the files on your own server rather than on their server and they will deliver them securely to your customers at only $10/month.

FetchApp seamlessly integrates with popular payment systems like PayPal and Shopify, and like Gumroad, it automates delivery of the digital goods for you securely via a downloadable link that you can can set to expire at a time that you determine or by number of downloads (or both).

FetchApp is another great way to sell your digital products that grows while your business grows!

26

KING SUMO - Create A "Viral" Contest to Build Your List Fast!

www.kingsumo.com
FREE

Now here's a very simple idea...

Want to get people to spread the word about your company? Have a contest and give away a grand prize!

It could be anything of value — an iPad, a "Dinner for Two" — maybe even a product or service you provide. It could be anything, but ideally, it should be something your ideal customer would want and need.

KingSumo creates a free "viral" contests for you and "gamifies" the process so that people are inspired to share the contest with their friends... and then they can share the contest with their friends... and they can share it with THEIR friends... and so on...

Contestants are inspired to tell their friends because the more people they tell, the more entries they get in the contest which means the better their chance of winning the prize!

Here's an interesting statistic: Did you know that if you can get 5 people to tell 5 people — and those five people tell five people, and this process happens **only 5 times**, that you have just reached **3,125 people!**

You can setup a contest in 10 minutes!

Here's how it works.

You upload the image, write the description of the prize, select a date for the contest to start and end and decide how many additional entries contestants will receive when they tell their friends on various platforms (they are allowed to enter the contest once each day).

Then you simply send the link they provide you with to your friends, your mailing list, add a link to the contest on your website, post the contest on social media and encourage people to tell their friends.

Throughout the contest KingSumo collects the names and email addresses of all the contestants for you so you can add them to your mailing list and market to them at a later time.

People can enter once each day to get more entries, and at the end of the contest KingSumo will show you the winner, you award the prize and download your new contact list!

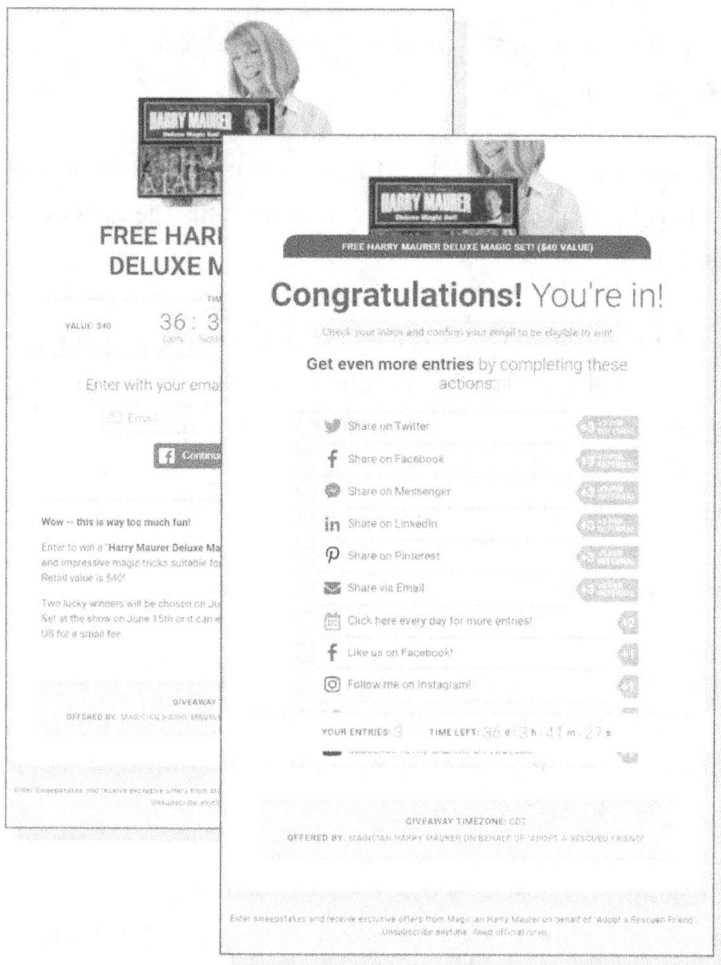

Be sure to send those that did not win a nice "thank you" email — or better yet, a discount coupon or consolation prize.

And now you have a list you can market to!

According to KingSumo, here's how effective these viral campaigns can be:

- **To get more email subscribers:** *New York Times* bestselling author Ryan Holiday used KingSumo to get 6,144 new email subscribers.

- **To get more social followers:** The Jeff Gordon NASCAR team used KingSumo to get 2,500+ new Instagram, Twitter, and Facebook followers.

- **To get more customers:** Degree 33, a surfboard company from California, used a giveaway to get 5,351 new leads — and generate $6,482.52 in revenue!

Hey — this is a great FREE and FUN way to get people onto your mailing list!

27

ADD THIS - Spread the Word About Your Company!

http://www.addthis.com/
FREE

This is a social sharing app that puts "share" buttons on your website allowing people to share your site with their social groups and has the ability for people to email your website link to their friends!

I used this service when they first popped onto the scene in 2006, and at the time, their program seemed limited so I stopped using it. I recently revisited it and was VERY impressed with what they now provide for FREE!

AddThis creates anchored buttons (below) or a floating button that appears on the side of your website and stays there as you scroll. It works on both

WordPress or HTML sites and you can configure it to "share" your site with others, or you can configure it to allow people to "follow" you on your various social media platforms.

It also has the ability to create "signup" forms that integrate with a variety of email systems (including MailChimp, Constant Contact and Aweber) and has a very easy to understand analytics that allows you to see how many people visited your site and how many people shared it with others.

I like it a lot!

28

ELEMENTOR - Build Your WordPress Website Yourself!

https://elementor.com/
FREE

I cannot tell you how many different WordPress website design programs I have tried and paid for until I discovered Elementor!

Elementor is the EASIEST mobile-responsive web page designer I have ever used and it is one of my "go-to" programs to create websites, various landing pages and more with very simple "drag-and-drop" features.

Do you want to add a video? – drag the icon in and add your YouTube link.

Do you want to add a headline or paragraph? – just drag it into place.

Installing it is simple and it comes complete with plenty of free templates to help get your creative juices flowing!

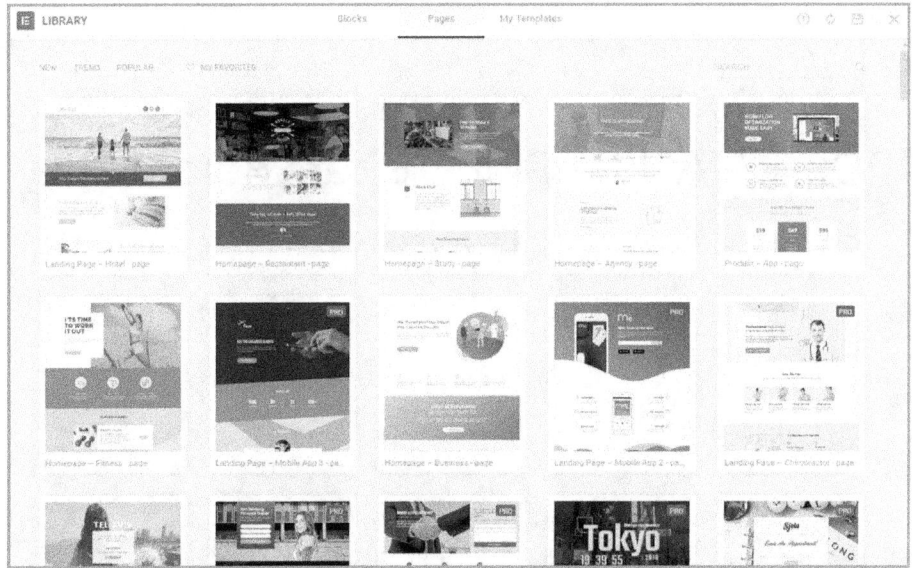

Elementor's FREE version is quite robust (and is the one I still use currently), but their full featured version is economical at only $49 for one site.

I do recommend also installing their free bare-bones WordPress theme called "Hello Elementor" which is a lightweight theme (the framework) that will allow your pages to open quickly (which has traditionally been a disadvantage of most WordPress sites).

You can download their bare bones theme here: https://wordpress.org/themes/hello-elementor/

29

POP-UP ALLY - Grab Visitors Before They Leave!

https://wordpress.org/plugins/popupally/
FREE (WordPress Plugin)

This is a WordPress plugin that puts attractive "signup forms" on your website. It also makes "exit pop-ups" (hence the name POPUP-Ally) that will encourage people to sign-up to your mailing list as they start to leave your site!

It's quick to configure, fast to install, takes zero technical skills, and can also create standard but stunning custom signup forms complete with an image or logo, so when people fill out the form it automatically subscribes them to your current autoresponder.

Although the pro version is $99/month, I have used their FREE version very effectively for one of my non-profit groups and it has worked wonderfully and created a LOT of new subscribers for them!

It does a really great job!

30

MEMO CHIMP - Add a "Sticky-Note" to your Website!

http://memochimp.com/
FREE!

This simple little program allows you to put a "Sticky Note" (like a "3-D" post-it note) on a web page.

It is a great, simple and eye-catching way to announce special deals and important announcements so they get noticed by your visitors!

To use it, you simply log into the free Memo Chimp service, type your message and then insert the code they give you onto your WordPress page or html page and the note will pop-up automatically!

You can even delay when the memo will appear, choose where on the page you would like the memo to show up, and you can even include a hyperlink in the memo itself if you like. (Visitors can close the sticky-note at anytime by simply clicking on the "x").

For HTML sites, you add a small piece of code to your web page.

If you are using this on a WordPress site, you will also need to install the "Free Monkey Plugin" that allows MemoChimp to work on Wordpress sites.

The link to the additional plugin is below:
http://monkeymarketingblog.com/

They also provide a clever way for you to have the link appear on the page without having to edit the page by creating a separate link to your page that will bring up the your web page with the memo attached (Perfect to include in an email)!

31

BRITE VERIFY - Keep Your Mailer Reputation High!

http://www.briteverify.com/
Low cost – A penny a name
(about $10 per 1,000 emails checked)

Although I now have a dedicated software that I use for this purpose (expensive), this is the one I started with and is the service I recommend to friends and clients. Although there is a cost involved (one penny per email checked), it is economical – after all, you may end up only cleaning your list about once a year to eliminate the "dead wood".

Cleaning your list of invalid emails is important!

When you send emails to invalid addresses they bounce. The more emails you bounce the lower your sender reputation will be with various email providers, and if your reputation gets too low, your emails will be deemed as "spam" and will be blocked and stop getting through, so it is important to keep your list clean.

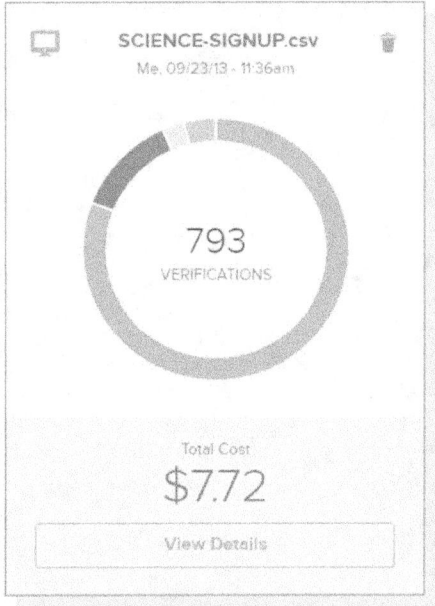

This service is really easy to use.

Just drag-and-drop your email list into BriteVerify and they will scan your list to show you the total number of records you uploaded and what the cost will be for cleaning in advance.

Then, at the click of a button your list is cleaned and you are provided with a display of your list.

The list will show you the number of emails that are valid, invalid and unknowns.

You can then download your newly cleaned list or download the invalid addresses and have your autoresponder delete them.

... A Clean List is a Happy List!

32

ENABLE MEDIA REPLACE - An Easy Way to Make WordPress Corrections

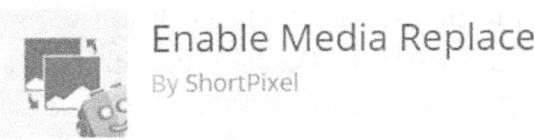

https://wordpress.org/plugins/enable-media-replace/
FREE (WordPress Plugin)

This plugin has proved invaluable to me and to some of the non-profits that I designed systems for.

It allows you to replace an image or a file in your WordPress media folder with another image or file WITHOUT having to change the link!

Imagine this scenario:

Imagine that you published a newsletter as a PDF file and stored it in your

WordPress media directory. You then sent an email with a link to the newsletter to thousands of people on your mailing list and then suddenly found a major mistake in your newsletter!

If you simply uploaded a corrected version of the newsletter into your WordPress media directory, WordPress would give the new file a new (different) link address. Those who tried clicking on the link you originally sent them would end up seeing the old version of the newsletter (or none at all if you deleted it).

This plugin allows you to actually replace the file (or image) in your media folder with another file without changing the web address, which allows you to easily replace one file for another.

It is also handy if you decide that you want to change an image that appears on a number of different web pages! Whether it is an updated head shot, a product image or a chart, by replacing the image with a new image using the same name, all pages will have the new image.

A lifesaver if you need to make corrections, change prices, charts, files or images on your WordPress website and more!

33

PHOTOPAD - Altering your Images can be a Breeze!

https://www.nchsoftware.com/photoeditor/kb/free.html
FREE — (Also available as a Windows 10 App)

If you do not currently have an image editing program, this one is simple and FREE (for non-commercial use). I still use it all the time because it is quick and easy!

If you ever tried using Photoshop (or the free equivalent "Gimp") you will quickly discover how complicated a process image editing can be! It can literally take you weeks to learn the basics of those programs when all you need to do is "resize" or "crop an image".

Simple to Crop a Photo!

The free version of PhotoPad has some advanced features that are easy to use including:

- Crop
- Resize
- Rotate
- Screenshot capture
- Straighten
- Resize
- Flip
- Change the background
- Vignettes
- Local Focus and blur areas
- Borders

- Text Panoramas
- ...and more

PhotoPad is extremely easy to use and, as I said, I use it myself all the time and recommend it to others for quick edits to crop, resize or adjust photos quickly.

34

ANIMOTO - Quick Short Videos in Seconds!

https://animoto.com
14 Day free trial
FREE For nonprofit organizations with approval
(https://animoto.com/business/non-profit)

Initially, I was not going to include this program in this book because they recently eliminated the free public version of their program that would have allowed you to create up to a 30 second promotional video at no charge.

But I decided to include it because they do offer a 14 day free trial which will allow you to create some videos for your use, and if you are a "non-profit organization" as of this writing with approval of your group's non-profit status, you will have the ability to create videos of any length at high resolution

(1080p) completely free!

Creating a video can be a laborious process for me, and to produce an edited video promotion that I am happy with can take me many hours!

(I once added up the time it took me to produce a 30 minute promotional video with many edits and it ended up taking me an average of one hour for each minute of video!)

After discovering this program, it made producing short promotional videos quick and easy.

Animoto takes no design skills and the entire video is created automatically in minutes from your photos and video clips!

The Editing Screen — just drop and click a button!

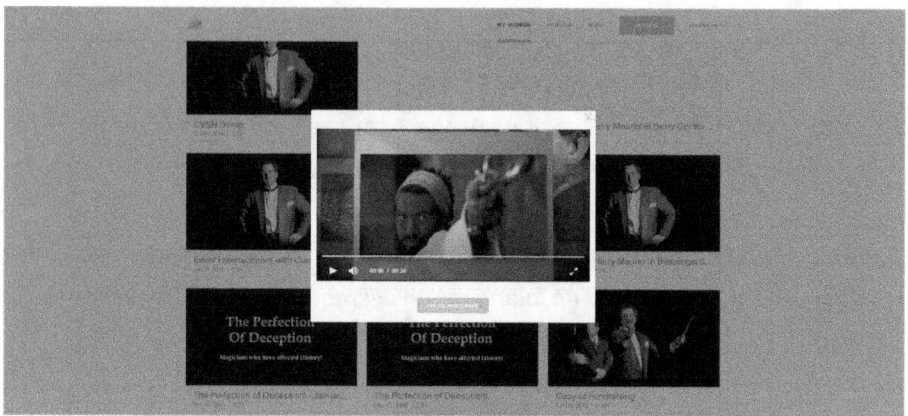

Your Finished Videos!

You simply select a video style, upload photos or videos clips to your account, put them in the order you would like them to appear, select music from their royalty free music library (or upload you own with voice overs if you would like), press a button, and Animoto will AUTOMATICALLY form the clips and images into an attractive video presentation for you! (No editing required!)

You will then have the options of embedding the video onto your web page, automatically uploading the video to YouTube, Facebook, Twitter – and more!

This is the perfect tool to add smart, short informative videos to your web page or landing page. And since it is so quick and easy to use – you can literally have your video online in minutes!

35

OPENSHOT - Slick Video Editing

https://www.openshot.org/
FREE

Want a FREE full-featured video editor?

Video editing programs can cost HUNDREDS of dollars!

OpenShot is an impressive video editor with TONS of editing features found in the most expensive software packages and includes various video effects, professional transitions, 3-D animations, titles, and a lot more!

I mentioned earlier that I don't necessarily enjoy video editing, but I find it necessary for my business and I have a few different video editing programs that I have paid for, but after reviewing this one — I think I may have spent money needlessly!

This program has all of the features my high-end programs have — and some great features my current programs are missing!

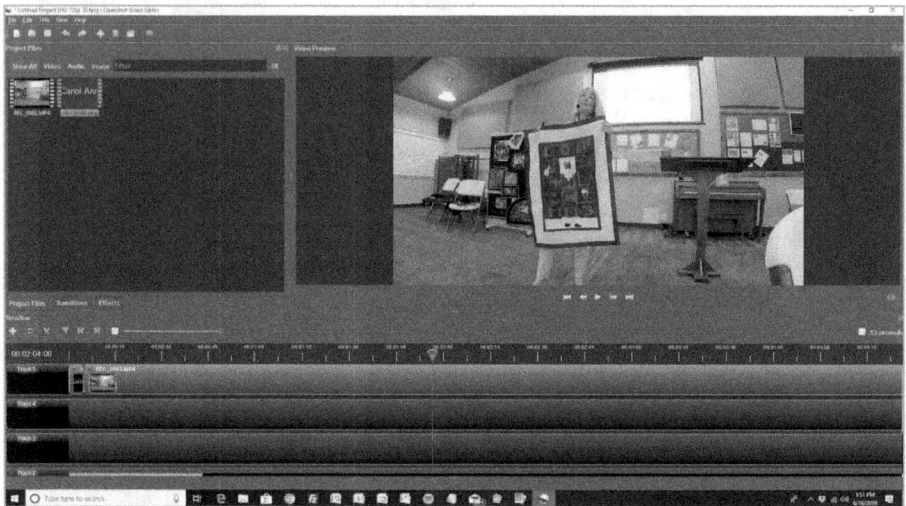

It is simple to use and to understand, and since it has a similar look and feel as my current go-to editor, there was virtually no learning curve!

Before spending money on a costly video editing program — try OpenShot. You may find that it has all the features you need, the ease of use you want and gives you the results you are looking for at no cost!

It is worth considering!

36

EVENTBRITE - Free Event Notifications!

https://www.eventbrite.com
FREE for no-cost events!

I don't want you to think that I don't like or appreciate EventBrite – It is a great service, but their costs are higher than some other services if you are SELLING tickets to an event. But if you are holding Free seminars, demonstrations, workshops or lectures – DEFINITELY consider using EventBrite!

When you are hosting a free event, you need to know how many people to expect in attendance so that you can arrange the seating, the food, printed materials, etc., and using a platform like EventBrite will give you an idea of how many people to expect at your event.

(Tip: Always anticipate that 10% more people will be attend your event...)

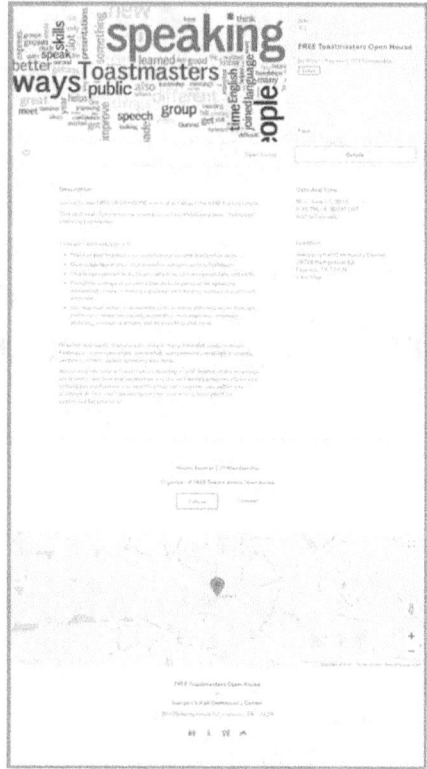

One advantage of using an event platform is that if you are advertising your event on the web, in print publications, or through flyers, you will be able to build your email list with those people who signup to your event. Obviously they have shown an interest and you can start a conversation with them after the event.

EventBrite's system is easy to use, the event invitations look slick and professional. You have the ability to upload your own contacts to send them invitations as well, and it allows you to see how many people you can expect through their RSVP process — and best of all…

For events where you are not charging a fee – it is FREE!

37

TICKET TAILOR - Ticketing for Live Events!

https://www.tickettailor.com/
LOW COST - $25/month (month to month) for up to 5 events
or an economical "pay-as-you go" option

If you are holding a "PAID" event like a seminar, show or lecture and need a ticketing system, I recommend "TicketTailor" — a very economical but full-fledged system for online ticketing.

TicketTailor has a very easy to use online ticketing system that will allow customers to purchase tickets at prices you set and you can even have "discount codes" that you can provide to purchasers.

Purchasers are taken to a ticketing page that you can customize.

ON YOUR OWN, BUT NOT ALONE!

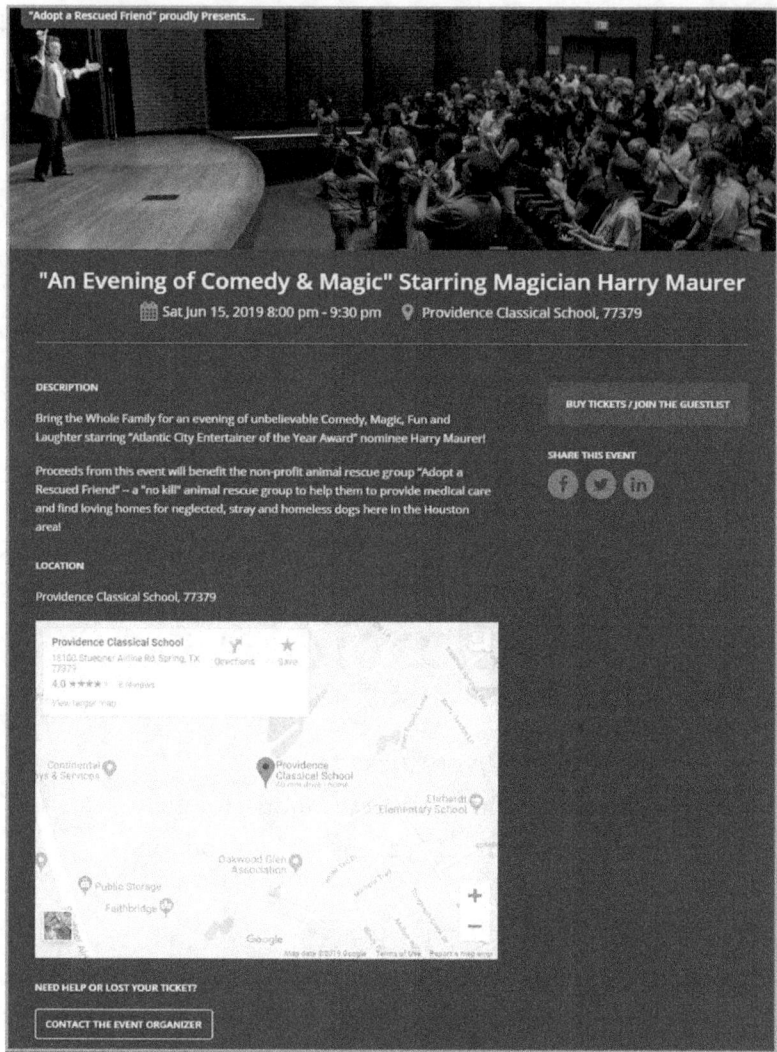

Once tickets are purchased they are sent to a page that they print off which is used as their ticket to the event (You can customize that page as well) and a copy of the ticket page is emailed to them as well.

On the night of the event, you can use either the TicketTailor's free automated ticket scanner app on your cell phone to check people in by scanning the QR code on their form, or you can print off an attendee list and check people in manually.

TICKET TAILOR - TICKETING FOR LIVE EVENTS!

The system is slick, professional and economical.

How economical?

Well, most online ticket platforms charge a "per-ticket" fee. TicketTailor has that option in their "Pay-as-you-go" plan, but they also have a better and simpler system that simply charges a flat monthly fee for the time that you have your tickets online for sale.

- Small events (up to 50 tickets) costs $25/month
- Medium Size event (up to 100 tickets) costs $45/month
- Large Event (up to 250 ticket sales) costs $99/month
- X-Large Events (up top 500 ticket sales) costs $175/month

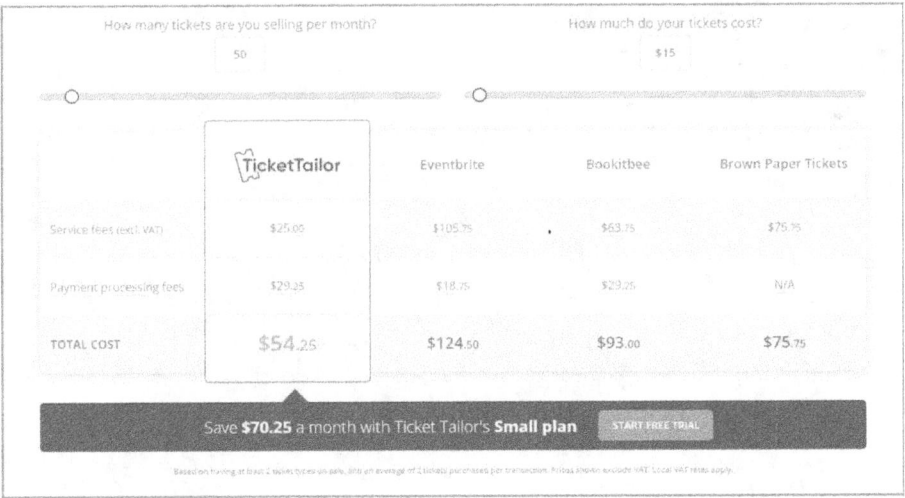

I suggested to this system to a friend who had been using EventBrite for his small venue that only seats 50 people for one show a week at a ticket price of $15/pp.

TicketTailor will only charge him $25/month for up to five events (that's his entire month's worth of shows) with as many as 250 tickets per event — without ANY ticketing fees! (As compared to: Eventbrite=$273, Picatic=$275, Bookitbee=$210).

A great savings – and he is not even a non-profit!

Non-profits are given a 20% savings on their plans, so if he were a non-profit, that fee would drop to only $17.50/month!

TicketTailor has a great online calculator so that you can easily see the savings as compared to other online providers.

I have used TicketTailor's ticketing program for my own theater programs and for my non-profit clients as well! — I highly recommend it!

38

LAST PASS - Never Forget a Password

LastPass •••|

https://www.lastpass.com/
FREE

With so many online services that you use on a day-to-day basis, it is important to be able to log on quickly to stay productive.

LastPass makes that easy by keeping all of your passwords securely stored in an online vault while allowing you to log onto your websites and services automatically!

First off, you should know that LastPass is a respected password manager rated highly by **PC Magazine**, **CNN Money**, **NPR**, **FOX Business** and the **New York Times** — so you should feel comfortable using it.

If you use Chrome, Firefox, Edge or nearly any major browser, LastPass attaches to your browser and you must first log into LastPass initially with a password you will not forget. (According to their online information — if you lose that master password, there is no way to retrieve it!)

Once you are logged into LastPass, when you first log onto any site, LastPass will ask you if you would like it to remember your login information for you. If so, then the next time you visit that same site, it will auto-fill the information for you into the sign-in box (or if you have more than one account, it will provide you with different login options) and you are able to log right in!

You can also save your credit card information and mailing address and at a press of a button it will fill the information in for you on various order forms.

Another benefit of using LastPass is that it is accessible on any of your devices.

If for some reason you are out of the office and need to log into a site from a remote computer, you can log into your LastPass account and log right into the site you wish to visit! (They even have a LastPass app so that you can log into sites from your phone.)

There are great benefits to using a password manager. First of all, you do not have to use a simple and easy to guess password — you can use very complicated passwords. And rather than trying to use the very same password for every site you visit, you can use a different and more complex password on each site keeping your accounts safe and secure.

I have used LastPass for over 10 years and can vouch for the time it has saved me.

As your business grows, you will find yourself using more services, apps, websites and programs — some of them infrequently — and it's great to know that you can log on quickly without having to memorize or search for a list of passwords.

I highly recommend LastPass for your security and productivity!

39

ZAPIER - Let Your Programs Talk to Each Other!

https://zapier.com/
FREE for 5 simple integrations

Wouldn't it be nice if your programs could talk to each other?

Zapier allows your web programs to tell each other what to do, and it does this without having to be a computer programmer.

The idea is that you create a workflow in Zapier (called a "Zap") telling it that when one program does something, it will trigger an action in another program.

ZAPIER - LET YOUR PROGRAMS TALK TO EACH OTHER!

Currently, Zapier integrates with over 1500 different online programs and services, so there is a good chance that programs you are currently using can talk to each other.

You can build you own customizations with their easy to use interface, or simply select an app from their list and Zapier will show you pre-programmed integrations that are ready to use!

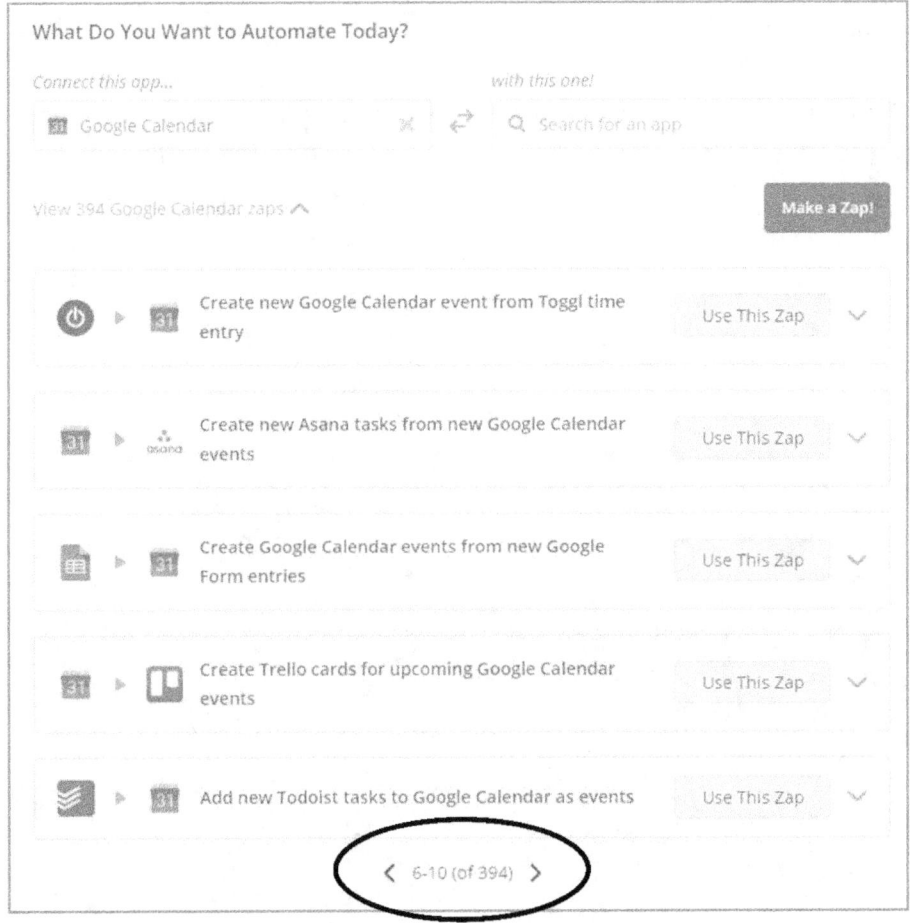

For example, just by typing "Google Calendar" into Zapier, it shows me 394 programs I can integrate it with!

With Zapier, I can create a Zap so that if someone fills out an online form on my site (using 123Forms mentioned in this book), I can have it automatically put that prospect's name and phone number on my Google Calendar on the following day for me to reach out to them!

That's just one example, but there are so many things you can do creating Zapier integrations, and unlike risking re-writing software code or hiring a programmer, you can easily try these integrations safely since they do not make any changes to your software, and if you are not happy with the zap you create — just delete it!

The Free version allows you to make 5 different integrations to create reliable systems that will save you time and create processes that will make your business more efficient.

40

FUNNELYTICS - See, Map and Plan Your Process!

https://app.funnelytics.io
Basic Version - FREE

Funnelytics allow you to graphically map out your sales processes visually!

Sure, you could use nearly any graphics program to draw boxes and arrows and make a simple representation of a sales process, but Funnelytics does this very easily for you. And to make your planning even easier, they also provide you with a swipe file of free funnel templates in their "Funnel Vault" just to help start you out.

In their "Funnel Vault", they provide free users with six pre-designed funnel models that you can use or adapt!

(NOTE: Their pro version is quite pricey, but at the time of this writing includes a total of 64 different funnel types that you can access.)

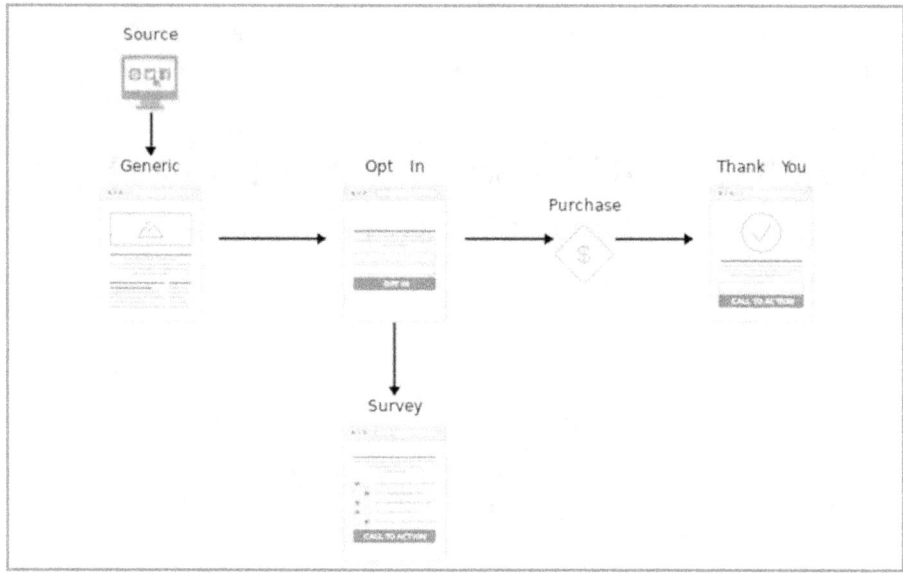

Funnelytics' Free Templates include:

1. LEAD MAGNET FUNNEL: Where you give something away (a "lead magnet") in exchange for their email address.

2. SURVEY FUNNEL: Where you can segment visitors and make different relevant offers based on the information they provided.

3. WEBINAR FUNNEL: Getting prospects to register for a webinar where you can then make them a special, limited time offer.

4. APPLICATION FUNNEL: Moving prospects through a three step process where you are able to pre-frame your program and get leads via a form or booking application.

5. **MINI-CLASS FUNNEL:** Where you get to educate prospects while selling your products.

6. **PRODUCT SALES FUNNEL:** Where you can qualify buyers by offering them an irresistible low ticket item, and afterwards offer them both "upsells" and "downsells" to increase the average cart value.

As I mentioned, their pro version is quite expensive (currently $695/year), but for that price, the program will allow you to put a script on each funnel's web page so that the program can analyze and track the results of your funnel for you automatically!

Some of things the pro version can track include:

- **People**: It tracks where people came from and what pages they visited.

- **Actions:** It tracks what actions people took — clicking a button, watching a video, etc.

- **Paths**: It tracks the paths that people took through your funnel.

- **Goals**: It will even track revenue for you!

But — putting the the tracking feature aside — just having the ability to plan your sales process out graphically and having proven templates to work from as a starting point makes this free resource both useful and valuable!

41

FUNNEL BUILDER - The Smartest Marketing Tool in Your Kit!

WELCOME TO THE ~~PAID~~ FREE DONE FOR YOU FUNNEL BUILDER

https://www.stephenesketzis.com/funnel-builder/
FREE

Seriously — marketers all over are charging $15,000 or more for a funnels like these, and when they find out that you can get them for FREE — they're going to be furious!

A Marketing or Sales Funnel is sales path a customer takes (whether online or offline) beginning with the "awareness" stage (when they first learn about your business) to the "purchase" stage (when they're ready to buy your product or service). When you build a funnel (which can be a series of web pages), you are creating the most effective path that customers will follow to make a purchase.

FUNNEL BUILDER - THE SMARTEST MARKETING TOOL IN YOUR KIT!

Before I explain about Funnel Builder, I would first like to recommend getting a copy of **"Dotcom Secrets"** by Russell Brunson. He is the developer of the most highly regarded (and expensive) funnel building platform around called "ClickFunnels" and he gives this book away FREE (plus shipping).

Yes, to get the book he cleverly uses a "Free Plus Shipping" marketing funnel to introduce you to ClickFunnels (the book is free — you just pay for shipping), but the book is fantastic and not only will you learn about funnels and how to design them yourself, but in the process, you will get to experience one of his marketing funnel when you order his book!

Here's the page to order "Dotcom Secrets": **https://dotcomsecrets.com**

Getting back to Funnel Builder...

Stephen Esketzis built this platform that helps you build eight different types of marketing funnels. They are:

- Webinar Funnel
- Free Plus Shipping
- Educational Bridge Funnel
- Membership Funnel
- Optin Funnel
- Product Sales Funnel
- Survey Funnel
- Product Launch Funnel

Of the eight types of funnels, you simply choose the funnel you would like to build, answer a few questions and then add your email address and the entire funnel is emailed right to your inbox.

ON YOUR OWN, BUT NOT ALONE!

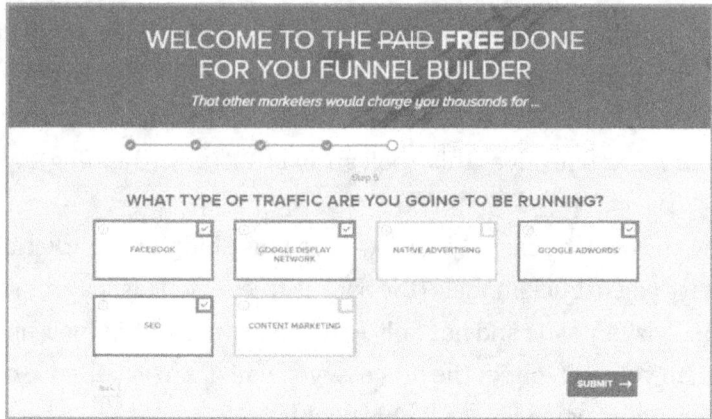

Now I will warn you that the funnel web pages themselves are designed to work with ClickFunnels which is a VERY expensive program (although they give you a 14 day free trial), but you can build these pages on your own with any web page program.

My suggestion would be to see samples of the funnel by viewing them in the link he provides and modeling them (the pages you will be looking for will be below the large video on the page he directs you to). You can also view samples of those funnel types in Funnelytics and build the pages in Elementor (both mentioned in this book).

He will also send you links in his email to various programs and services that you may or may not consider using.

The most valuable things that you will receive with any of the funnels you choose are:

- The ClickFunnels preview of your funnel.

- The "Screenshot Swipe Vault" which shows you the layout of various pages (it is free to signup to get into the vault).

- The Pre-written emails to edit (which are sent as attachments to the email you will receive).

- The templates for your "giveaway" (also sent as attachments).

- and the link to the free training at ClickFunnels University - a wonderful training resource!

And all of this information, samples, education and copy writing — is Free!

42

TRELLO - Get Organized and Plan your Business...Visually!

www.trello.com
FREE

I learned about Trello from a Frank Kern presentation where he was using it as a sales example — and I was impressed!

You can probably tell by now that I like to see things visually, and Trello does that for you!

With Trello you create an online board that you can share with team mates (with a link) and you add cards to the board in columns (like virtual file cards) which you can move, reorder and add to as the project progresses.

TRELLO - GET ORGANIZED AND PLAN YOUR BUSINESS...VISUALLY!

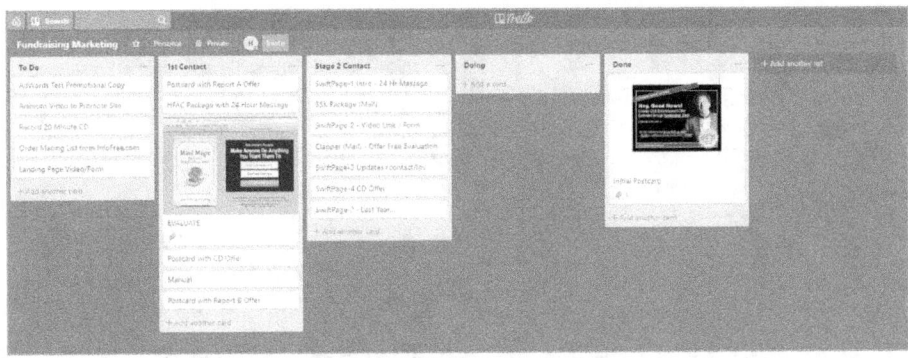

But unlike file cards pinned onto a cork board, you can open each card and add photos, links, documents, schedule due dates and any related information to any of the cards.

And if you are on the road and have a sudden "flash of inspiration", you even have the ability to send an email to the "board" (they give you an email address) and the subject line of your email becomes the title of a new card and the body of the email becomes the content!

It is a great free planning tool for you and your team to use to plan marketing campaigns, product launches or any project that you want to see in a movable, flexible and visual list.

43

TODOIST - Get Things Done!

https://todoist.com
FREE

Todoist is more than just a "to do" list.

This is a top rated planning app used and endorsed by **NASA, Harvard University** and **Netflix**!

It keeps your projects and tasks organized in list form and and allows you to prioritize your tasks according to due dates and importance (ala Stephen Covey) while allowing you to assign tasks to different members of your team.

Their free version allows you to create up to 80 projects with an unlimited number of tasks per project with up to 5 team members per project — more than enough for any small business.

TODOIST - GET THINGS DONE!

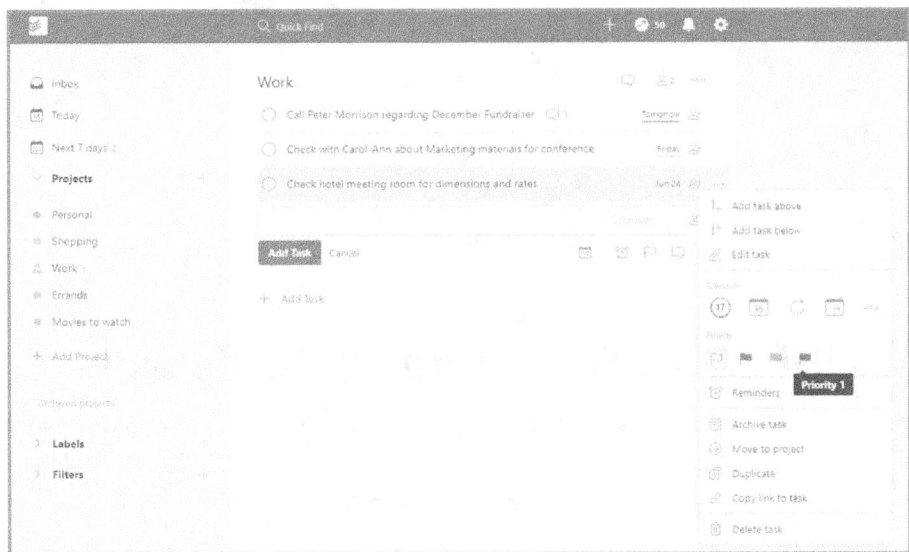

Todoist can be viewed on your computer, your phone or any mobile device. And unlike a lone "to do" list, with Todoist you and your team members can collaborate and leave comments on various tasks and projects.

Conveniently, your Todoist tasks will be emailed to you as well — no reason for things to fall through the cracks!

If you are currently using a "to do" list — consider moving up to something more useful and collaborative.

44

BUBBL.US - Brainstorming Made Simple!

https://bubbl.us/
FREE for 3 Mind Maps

Visually Plan your Campaigns, Thoughts and Ideas!

Mind mapping is a way of visually planning out a project, business or idea on paper.

In its traditional form, you are encouraged to take a large sheet of paper (8-1/2" x 11" is too small) and starting with a central theme, you work outward connecting steps together until you have a paper loaded with creative thoughts and ideas and you have filled in all of the gaps connecting the steps you will need to make to complete your project.

It's a visual thinking tool for structuring information to help you better understand, remember and generate new ideas.

Well, the digital age has caught up to the pencil and paper!

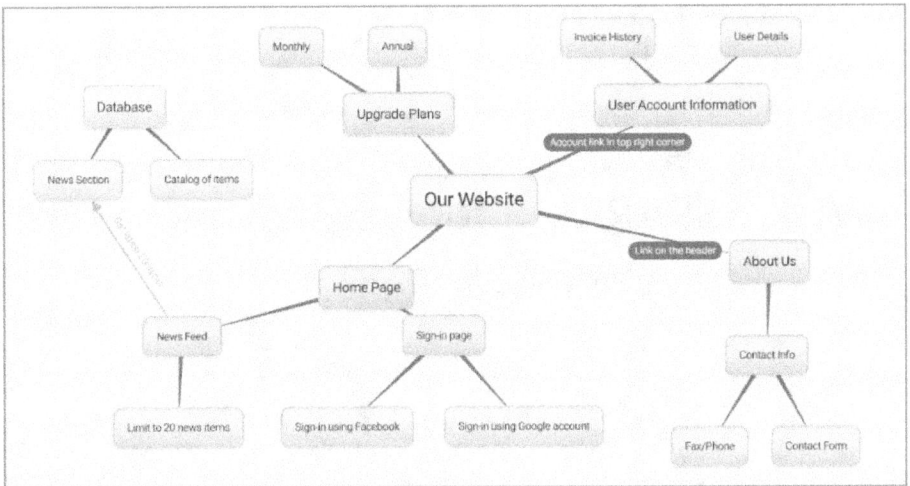

Bubbl.us allows you to mind map right on your computer, and unlike a paper version where you will be constantly erasing, crossing out, redrawing (and at times starting over and over again), the virtual space is limitless and your steps can be moved or deleted with ease.

It is a thinking man's tool, and as a business owner, you will be coming up with business ideas, marketing systems, products, service designs and more regularly, and a tool like this is extremely helpful.

With Bubbl.us's "Free Forever Plan" you can create up to 3 different mind maps (you can always print them off and create new ones) and if you choose to upgrade to their paid plan for $59/year you can add files, collaborate with others, see your revisions and allow others to edit your mind map.

I think you will agree that the free version may be all that you will need to plan your projects visually.

45

WHITESPARK - 3 tools to Advance your Google Reach

https://whitespark.ca/
FREE

If someone has a YouTube account, if they have a Gmail account, if they have a Google+ account, or if they use any Google applications like Google Docs, Google Maps, or a Google Calendar — then they have a Google account, so it would be safe to say that a majority of your customers or prospects have Google accounts — and if they do, they can be encouraged to help you promote your business!

Whitespark is a Canadian company that builds tools and provides services to help businesses and agencies with local search marketing and they provide some very useful free tools to help you with your marketing efforts.

Feel free to explore their site, but the three Free tools I really like are:

LOCAL CITATION FINDER

https://whitespark.ca/local-citation-finder/

A Citation is any mention of your business on the web (with or without a link). It is any combination of your company name, phone number, address, zip or postal code.

Citations are important for local search rankings as they verify that a business exists, established trust, and creates prominence.

Just by entering a few items into a form, Whitespark's Free Local Citation Finder will show you the results of your online presence — and if you wish — the results of your competitor's online presence.

It takes just a minute to enter the information and a link to the results are emailed to you.

Although it is not a complete listing, it will give you a simple overview of your positioning.

GOOGLE REVIEW GENERATOR LINK

https://whitespark.ca/google-review-link-generator/

If you have a free Google Business Listing (and why wouldn't you?), this simple page will provide you with a link to send to your customers so that you can encourage them to post an online Google Review of your business. Perfect to include with a thank you email to your customers.

GOOGLE REVIEW HANDOUT!

https://whitespark.ca/review-handout-generator/

By entering just a few details, this page will automatically create a printable flyer for you to insert in shopping bags or hand to customers which will provide them with instructions on how to post a review of your business on Google once they get home.

46

62 STOCK IMAGE SITES - Images at Your Fingertips!

bit.ly/62StockImages
FREE

OptimizePress is a very good web page design program — I do own it and have used it in the past, but this link that they provide (publicly) is a wonderful resource to help you find free quality stock images that you can use in your websites, flyers and promotions.

On this page they include a list of 64 different websites where you can search for high-quality images to use at no cost!

OptimizePress also takes a moment to explain why using images in your promotions are so important and they even go though the details of explaining various usage rights so that you understand the proper way to use stock images legally.

A sample image from PLiXS (one of their recommended websites)

It is a great resource, and with so many sites included, and such a variety of styles and images to choose from, this is a page you will want to bookmark and use when you are planning your promotional designs.

As one viewer said in her online comments, *"OMG I am in image heaven!"*

47

PHOTOFUNIA - A Way to be Creating and Fun!

http://photofunia.com/
FREE

This is both fun — and useful!

Performing image editing and applying picture effects to any image is a time consuming exercise that is fit only for an avid PhotoShop user.

This program lets you do it instantly — and it's FREE!

ON YOUR OWN, BUT NOT ALONE!

- Want to put your image on the side of building? — No problem!
- Want to see your photo on an artist's sketchpad? — Easy!
- Want to see your company's name on a "tattoo"? — Takes a second!

Here are just some of the effects and a sample that I did in seconds by selecting an image from my computer and clicking "go"

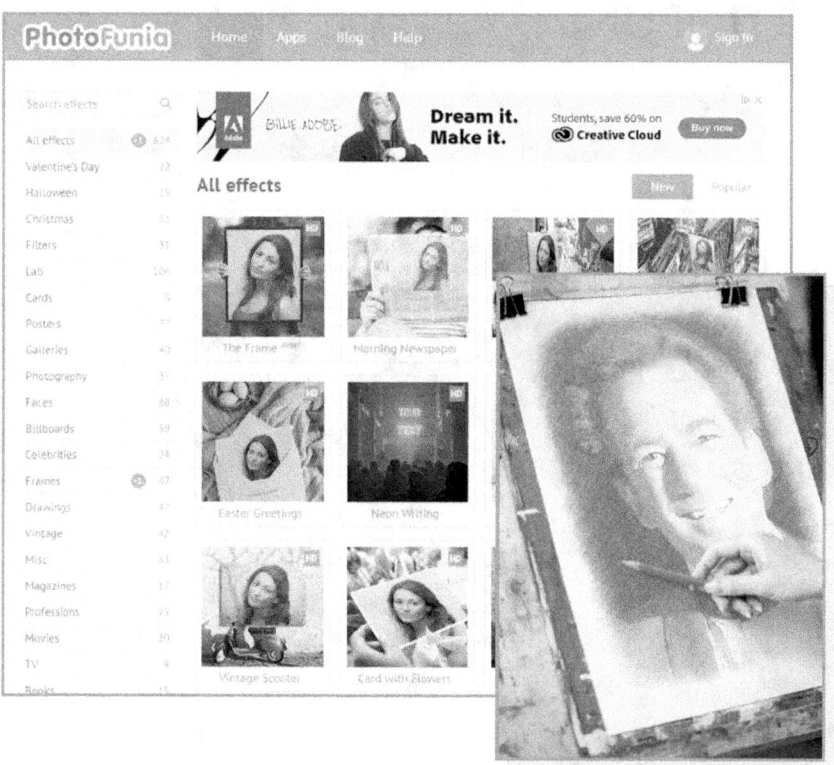

There are effects using images (or just text if you prefer) and these final images are perfect to use in social media, email promotions, flyers, website images and more.

Fast, Fun and FREE! — how can you beat it!

48

POSTER MY WALL - Professionally Designed Posters, Videos & Graphics

postermywall

https://www.postermywall.com
Flyer & Poster Designs = $2.99 - $7.99
Videos = $14.95 - $24.95
Printed 20 x 30 = $17.95
24 x 36 posters= $24.95

If you are not necessarily artistically inclined — or if you are short on time — or if you need professional inspiration and designs, this site will allow you to design professional looking flyers and posters (and even promotional videos) that can be used for Facebook ads and website promotions!

Best of all, they are all economically priced!

Having a sale, promoting a service or product or announcing an event ?

You simply select a template, make whatever adjustments you would like to make on the template, and when you are happy with your final design, you can download a sample (with a watermark) for demo purposes or to show colleagues. When you are ready, you can download the final version ready for printing in various resolutions depending upon your needs for a very small and fair price!

If you would like a professionally printed copy of your posters or flyers, you can do that online too! Not just on paper (single sided or double-sided), but on window clings, removable wall adhesive posters — and even banners!

Videos Too!

Do you need to create a video ad or an eye-catching video for your website or social media page? Poster My Wall lets you easily create engaging videos — no experience needed! Like their posters and flyers, when you are happy with the results, you pay a small fee to download the finished project!

Simple to use, quick to produce and economical to use.

I think you will be very impressed — (I know I am!).

49

WAVE VIDEO - Create Short Promotional Videos!

https://wave.video/
FREE: 15 second videos at 750p in two different formats
(Paid Plans start at $8.25/month for videos up to 1 minute in length in various formats)

15 Seconds may not sound like a lot of time, but may be perfect length to catch viewers attention in Facebook posts and Facebook ads, and with videos being so popular and with YouTube now being the second largest search engine in the world — posting videos on YouTube will help with your online ranking!

With Wave.Video you can use your own video clips or choose from over 200 million stock videos and images that they provide in their library to produce a finished video with text animations, your company logo and more in two different layouts — landscape or square mode (ideal for social media).

Wave.Video's editing platform is simple to use, and adding text and images is a breeze! You can literally edit one of their video templates in minutes with very professional results.

Cleverly, they also provide you with a "Social Calendar" filled with ideas throughout each month that you can use as inspiration to produce videos for various Holidays. Not just obvious days like "Christmas" and "Fathers Day", but obscure holidays like "International Surfing Day", and "National Daiquiri Day" — things that will get your creative juices flowing!

Why not give video marketing a try?

Even if you don't have video footage of your own to use yet, with their stock footage, your text, and their simple to use editor, you can create tons of videos highlighting your business that you can be proud of!

50

WONDERSHARE STREAMING - Don't Waste Your Most Productive Times!

https://www.wondershare.com/pro/streaming-audio-recorder.html
Normally $29, but available for a limited time for $19

Research is a vital part of any business. I read business books and listen to webinars and online training a lot! (Hey, if you are not growing, you are dying!)

Webinars, Seminars, Podcasts, Online Classes and YouTube videos are all informative, but do you really want to spend the most productive business time that you have available to idly watch a webinar — especially when by the end you may discover that the webinar was not up to snuff?

I listen to an average of about four webinars a week on different subject —

mostly marketing, but some on fundraising, self-improvement and others on newly developed software programs that I may find useful.

Unfortunately, most of those webinars are held in the middle of my working day, so rather than waste the prime times I have watching or listening to them — I record them instead!

Now if you have ever tried recording a webinar or an online class or anything from a streaming service, you may find that service like "GoToWebinar" or "Stitcher" are intentionally designed to not allow your computer to record them.

Yes, there are some complicated "workarounds" to that...

You can run a cable from the speaker output of your computer to the microphone input and then using a recording software, adjust the sound appropriately and then wait for the webinar to start and press "Record" and then hopefully you will be able to catch the end of the webinar in time to stop the recording — otherwise you have to manually edit the captured audio manually. (It's a labor intensive process.)

But there's a better way!

I use **Wondershare's Streaming Audio Recorder**.

There are other computer programs available that will allow you to bypass the recording limitations that I mentioned, but there is **ONLY ONE** (that I know of), that not only bypasses those limitations by recording directly from the sound card to your computer, but can be set to "listen" and record once the program starts and then after hearing a prolonged silence, it will stop recording automatically!

I can't tell you what a blessing and time saver this has been and how productive this has allowed me to be while still getting the education I desire!

Just open the webinar window and open Wondershare Audio Recorder and press record and it sits and waits while you work, and when the webinar starts and someone starts speaking, the program will automatically start recording by itself, and when it finishes and hears prolonged silence (a length at which you can adjust) — it stops!

Be forewarned that some Webinar programs need you to "click" on the screen before they will begin playing or streaming — so in rare cases you might have to be there at the start of the webinar to start it off, but after that, you can turn the volume down and work on your business on other screens knowing that Wondershare will stop recording on its own when the webinar finishes.

Once the recording has finished, you are able to label the recording right inside the program with the title and the artist/presenter and other details, and when ready, you can listen to the recording right inside Wondershare or you can download your MP3 recordings onto a USB drive or burn them onto a CD and listen to them at your convenience.

I am sure you are asking: "Since webinars are a visual medium, do I miss any of the content that is being presented?"

From my experience, unless it is a highly visual presentation showing graphic layouts or how to use a piece of software, I may miss some of the content, but in most cases I have not missed a thing by "listening" rather than "watching" these presentations.

<u>**At the moment the software is discounted at $19**</u> — but even at the full price of $29, it is well worth the cost for the education I have gained, the time I have saved, and the sales I have made while those webinars were being recorded!

Wondershare Audio Recorder allows me to focus and work during my work day, and then during my time on the road — either in the car or on a plane — I can listen with my full attention to those recordings at a time that is convenient **to me!**

In Conclusion...

In case you don't think that these programs are genuinely useful you should know that I used the following resources for the creation of this book and for the associated online information:

- I used **Reedsy** to write and layout this book and make it ready for publication.
- I used **Canva** to design the book's cover.
- I used **Funnelytics** to plan the process I will use to market and promote this book.
- I used **NameSilo** for my domain registration.
- Some simple graphic edits I did in **PhotoPad.**
- I added **PopupAlly** and **AddThis** to my website to help build my mailing list.
- I used **Hubspot** for the marketing database for subscribers of this book and for my lecture contacts.
- I used **MailerLite** as my autoresponder for my community.
- I used **KingSumo** to help get the word out about the pre-publication of this book.
- I used **MemoChimp** to add quick pre-publication "sticky notes" to my website.
- I used **Photofunia** to create the pencil drawing on the "Author" page.
- I used **Gumroad** as the selling platform for the digital version of this book.

And that's just for this project!

IN CONCLUSION...

Some of the additional programs that I use in my business all the time include: **Faxaway, Calendly, SocialBFF, Shortkeys, LastPass, Ninite, GetEmail, Zapier, TicketTailor, Animoto, Elementor, Enable Media Replace, Kunaki, NinjaForms, 123formbuilder** — and lots of Google programs!

So if you had any doubts about the usefulness of these tools and programs, you can be assured that these programs will work just as well in your business as they do in mine. I mean, if I can use them effectively with just this project, imagine what you can do with them to help you to start or build your business — all at no (or little) cost!

I would like to thank a few people who were helpful and generous with their suggestions and time. My wife Carol Ann who is always supportive and helped edit and point out areas that might need more clarification to non-technical people. My high school and college buddy Steven Friedlander who immediately came up with the perfect title for this book, and many of my friends and family who were excited about this book even before it was published!

I would also like to invite you to join my Private Facebook Group at **http://bit.ly/OnYourOwnFB** where we will share updates, new tools and resources with our community.

Enjoy and use these resources — I wish you great success!

Review Request

If you enjoyed this book and found it useful, I would be very grateful if you'd post an honest review on Amazon.

Your support really does matter and it really does make a difference. I do read all the reviews and I do make changes as a result of that feedback.

If you'd like to leave a review then all you need to do is go to the review section on this book's Amazon Page. You'll see a big button that says "Write a Customer Review" — click on that and you're good to go!

Here's the page if you need it:
https://www.amazon.com/dp/B082H6WTZ3/

Thanks for our support.

Wishing you much success!

HARRY MAURER

About the Author

Harry Maurer has been involved in one of the most unique and difficult businesses to succeed in — Harry is a professional entertainer, and surprisingly, unlike many in his field, since he was a child he has never held another job.

As a much-in-demand entertainer, he travels the world extensively performing in casino showrooms in Las Vegas and Atlantic City, entertaining in luxury resorts in exotic places and thrilling audiences aboard the very top cruise lines around the world!

Much of his success has to do not just with his ability to consistently entertain audiences, but his knowledge and expertise at marketing himself, and like any solo-entrepreneur he needed to find very specific tools to make his business grow.

There was a logical process he would follow to find programs to help his business.

First he would explore free and low-cost options. If they did what he wanted them to do, he would then consider upgrading to more expensive versions from the developer. If they did not perform up to his expectations, he would find better programs from other vendors having a better idea of what he was looking for.

After finding free and low-cost tools as alternatives to thousands of dollars worth of programs, software and services and after sharing these tools with friends, groups and organizations, he had a revelation and determined that if for some reason he had to start a business from scratch — or wanted to help a struggling business succeed— then these are the programs and resources he would use.

Each of the resources in this book are free or low cost, but they are all high-quality programs that do exactly what they are supposed to do (and many of these programs he still uses today!).

Harry Maurer continues to entertain internationally throughout the year and between his award-winning performances, he schedules engaging lectures around the country.

As he finds more interesting programs, he shares them with his followers.

To contact Harry Maurer:
ON CUE PRODUCTIONS
   18062 FM 529, Suite 176
   Cypress, TX 77433-1168
   (281) 345-9322
   harry@hmmagic.com

You can connect with me on:

🌐 https://www.hmmagic.com
📘 http://bit.ly/OnYourOwnFB
🔗 https://www.linkedin.com/in/hmmagic

www.ingramcontent.com/pod-product-compliance
Lightning Source LLC
Chambersburg PA
CBHW032123250526
R18348000001B/R183480PG45466CBX00048B/15